15th Oct '91.

Winston & Doreen,

Each time I visit your home
I leave refreshed in body, mind,
and spirit. Thank you both.

Alan. & Irene

A THOUSAND MILES OF MIRACLE

A personal record of God's delivering power in China

by
ARCHIBALD E. GLOVER

Abridged by
L.T. LYALL

Foreword by
J.C. POLLOCK

Foreword to the 1991 edition by
DAVID J. MICHELL

AN OMF CLASSIC

© OVERSEAS MISSIONARY FELLOWSHIP
(*formerly China Inland Mission*)
Published by Overseas Missionary Fellowship (HQ) Ltd.,
2 Cluny Road, Singapore 1025
Republic of Singapore

First published 1904
Twenty-second edition 1957
This Edition 1991

OMF BOOKS *are distributed by*
OMF, 10 *West Dry Creek Circle, Littleton*, CO 80122, USA
OMF, *Belmont, The Vine, Sevenoaks, Kent*, TN13 3TZ, UK
OMF, *PO Box* 177, *Kew East, Victoria* 3102, AUSTRALIA
OMF, 1058 *Avenue Road, Toronto, Ontario* M5N 2C6, CANADA
OMF, *PO Box* 10159 *Balmoral, Auckland*, NEW ZEALAND
OMF, *PO Box* 41, *Kenilworth* 7745, SOUTH AFRICA
and other OMF offices.

ISBN 9971-972-95-6
Printed in Singapore

CONTENTS

The Rev. Archibald E. Glover, M.A.

FOREWORD TO THE 1991 EDITION

NO one dreamed that the shadows of the year that ushered in the twentieth century would fall forward and fall so darkly.

In China 1900 is remembered for the Boxer Rebellion. The annals of church and missionary history record that 181 missionaries and children and over 49,000 Chinese Christians were martyred. Among the missions, the China Inland Mission lost the largest number — 58 missionaries and 22 children.

These nine decades since the terrifying year of 1900 have stamped this century as the one bringing the greatest antagonism to Christianity and the greatest suffering since the birth of the Christian Church. Widespread persecution continues today in many lands, for religious, political, nationalistic, ideological and spiritual reasons.

Subsequent to the dramatic events of this book, Chinese Christians have faced continuing persecution in the turmoil and travail of such events as the founding of the Republic in 1912, the 1927 revolution, the Long March of the 1930s, the Sino-Japanese conflict of 1937-45, the communist takeover of 1948-49, the Cultural Revolution 1966-70 and the Tiananmen Massacre of June 4, 1989.

Faith in God and the evidence of God's faithfulness have shone through Christians' trials and tears through the years. A Thousand Miles of Miracle, the true story of

Archibald and Flora Glover's 67 harrowing days, is undoubtedly one of the most remarkable records of triumph in tragedy.

The Overseas Missionary Fellowship is reprinting this testimony of God's keeping power in the 125th anniversary year of the founding of the CIM. It shows faith to be enthusiastic adhesion to the living Christ, no matter how adverse the circumstances, and faith in God alone to be the real thing when all other supports have gone.

We believe that as the twenty-first century approaches, this message is more relevant and urgent for more Christians than ever before.

OMF Director for Canada   David J Michell

FOREWORD

IN 1900 the world, not yet inured to horrors, and taking
for granted that if British subjects were molested overseas the Royal Navy would demand the reason why,
was startled by news of massacre in China.

Of the missionaries and their children martyred before
the Boxer Rising was suppressed, after the landing of an
International Expeditionary Force and heavy fighting
around Peking, seventy-nine were of the China Inland
Mission. All through that exceptionally hot summer small
parties of missionaries made their way towards the safety
of Treaty Ports, experiencing appalling distresses and
seeing colleagues murdered or dying of ill-treatment and
exposure. One of the survivors was the Reverend Archibald Edward Glover, a Church of England clergyman in
early middle age who, with his young wife and two small
children, had joined the China Inland Mission shortly
before, after nine years' ministry in England.

The Boxer Rising was soon forgotten in greater world
tragedies and tumults; its only traces the memories of
participants or loot from the Summer Palace—I am afraid
there is some in possession of my family. But out of it
came a classic of Christian experience: this book. Before
Archibald Glover died in 1954 at the great age of ninety-
five, it had passed through twenty-one editions in
English, and been translated into German, Swedish,
Danish and Arabic. The original was somewhat overlong
and Mr. Lyall's abridgement and his introductory

chapter, "The Shadow of an Agony", makes it available to a new generation, ensuring a further and prolonged lease of life.

Glover said, forty years after the book's publication, that though "written originally to strengthen the faith of the people of God who are called for Christ's sake and the Gospel's to suffer affliction, yet it has pleased Him to use it in a quite remarkable way to the arresting and converting of unbelievers and, very notably, of infidels and agnostics". This is not surprising, for it is "a plain, unvarnished narrative of a humanly desperate situation on the one hand, and of a Divinely miraculous salvation on the other".

A number of lessons stand out. The first, perhaps, is the cost of Christian service. Not all are called to endure as the Glovers, but all must be ready. The account unfolds of stifling rooms and hostile crowds, of the agony of travel as prisoners on springless trollies, deliberately driven along the roughest part of the road; of the scorching heat of the hill top, of the stripping, "by a painful process not far removed from lynching", which left Glover, his wife (who was expecting her third baby and was in no condition to travel even in comfort) and their children almost naked in the hands of brutal and licentious peasants. All this was for Christ. As little Hedley Glover said, when they were made to sleep in the filth and stench of a beggar's platform, "I think Jesus must have slept in a place like this when He had nowhere to go. . . . We ought to be glad that we are like Jesus."

Yet Glover is not ashamed to admit to human weakness. There is no pretence. He tells of fears, of terror when they

heard that they were sentenced to be torn in pieces. He
cries out in anguish, as any husband would, when he sees
his wife set upon by angry men. Sometimes the sense of
God's presence is overwhelmingly strong but at others
the pressure of hunger, exposure and awful uncertainties
brings deep depression: "that hallowed sense of our Lord's
presence . . . was now withdrawn". But the story of Miss
Gates, kneeling by Mrs. Glover, prostrate and in darkness
of soul under the pitiless sun, and pouring into her ear
"passage after passage, promise after promise, exalting
His name, declaring His faithfulness", until Flora Glover,
"with tears coursing down her cheeks, said 'Oh, I will
never doubt again' ", and they sing together, with cracked
lips and tongues scarcely moving, "How sweet the name
of Jesus sounds", must be one of the most moving incidents
in missionary literature.

The loyalty of Chinese Christians, who risked torture
and death, and the kindness of unknown and unexpected
Chinese friends whispering words of comfort or bringing
food, should not be forgotten.

The overriding, dominant impression of this narrative
is of the reality of God's personal intervention.

He guides. He succours. He restrains the malice of
enemies. He intervenes through the forces of nature. The
Glovers—and at times their oppressors—are left in no
doubt that there is a God in Heaven and that the living
Christ by His Spirit is with them. Again and again at
desperate moments they see His hand. Once it is an enemy
who, intending mischief, in fact brings them on their
way; once it is a sympathetic soldier. The Bible, not
surprisingly, is a lamp to their feet: ". . . Then the words

in verses 1 and 8 lighted up. . . . The call was so clear
and emphatic that I felt convinced that flight was now for
us a God-appointed duty." On another occasion there is
a strong inward urge, such as He gives His servants now
and again: "All the old sense of helplessness came over
me. But, as my wife and I were pleading with God for
our sister's recovery, I heard a voice as distinctly as if it
were spoken in my ear—'Up get thee down and tarry
not!' The impression was so deep and I so certain that
God had spoken. . . ." A few minutes, and they would
have been too late.

The power of the indwelling Holy Spirit stands out
from these pages. Prayer is the spontaneous reaction to
every need. And God is not limited by the feebleness of
faith: "As we prayed, I fear my faith was hardly prepared
for the answers God vouchsafed to our prayers. The
impossible to us was again proved to be possible for Him."
Moreover, they are given "grace sufficient to endure the
heat and the cravings of hunger and thirst . . . as well as
a forbearing spirit and courteous manner towards those
who thrust themselves so rudely upon us or plied us with
contemptuous questions". Could they, physically and
mentally at the end of their tether, have been courteous
under such treatment were the Spirit of the Lord Jesus
Himself not in their hearts? And they can proclaim the
Gospel. A bad man would be resentful, a good man might
be depressed, a religious man resigned; but these, because
they are His, pass on the Word of Life.

Above all, *A Thousand Miles of Miracle* is proof of the
Gospel. "To find it possible to be possessed at such a
time", writes Glover, "by the spirit of divine love and

compassion, instead of the natural spirit of resentment and hate, was to us a tangible evidence of the truth of the Gospel we had preached, such as no philosophy in the world could explain away."

The Glovers were very ordinary people; but they had believed in and proclaimed a Risen, Living Christ. It had been easy, perhaps, in the quiet security of a Gloucester-shire curacy or with the aristocratic, unruffled congrega-tion of St. Paul's, Onslow Square. Almost as easy, no doubt, among the converts and on the street corners of Luan, especially with Stanley Smith of the Cambridge Seven as your senior. But now? Stripped, robbed and hurt, facing a degrading death and, worse, your little boy exposed to possible slavery, your little girl to rape. Falsely accused of disgusting crimes, by those for whom you had left all. Do the truths you believe still hold water?

This book gives the answer, overwhelming and irresistible.

HORSINGTON, SOMERSET.   J. C. POLLOCK.

THE SHADOW OF AN AGONY

FEBRUARY, in the year 1900, was bitterly cold on the wide, wind-swept plateau of south-east Shansi. Light snow sometimes fell but never covered the brown expanse of good earth for long. The chief or prefectural city of this prosperous agricultural area was Luan, the approach to which, either from Hungtung in the Fen River valley to the west or from the important city of Shunteh to the north-east was along dry, stony, river valleys and through rugged, sparsely populated mountain country. It needed five or six days' hard travelling in either direction on mule back or by mule litter—the common modes of transport.

Luan was opened as a centre for missionary work throughout this populous plain by Mr. C. T. Studd and Mr. Stanley Smith of "Cambridge Seven" fame. Mr. Stanley Smith was the missionary-in-charge in 1896 when the Rev. Archibald Glover, an Oxford man, together with his wife, arrived from England to join him. The contrast between Victorian England and the primitive interior of China was even greater then than between England and China today. Hedley, their first child, was born soon after their arrival at Luan and Hope came to join him the following year.

The mission station lay on the broad main street of the city near to the massive north gate. The high walls had been the city's protection for two or three thousand years. Life inside and outside the walls had changed very little with the passage of time. The farmers in their mud-walled cottages and villages sowed their wheat each autumn in anticipation of the spring rains. The winter was long and then, with amazing suddenness, the warm winds and heavy rains of April would set everything growing apace. Acacia trees burst into blossom, filling the air with their pungent fragrance. Bees hummed around the thorny but sweet-smelling date trees. Apricot and then peach trees burst into blossom. The wheat sprang up, ripened and was ready for harvest in June. No sooner was the wheat gathered in than the summer rains fell in torrents, preparing the way for the autumn crops of maize, millet and sorgum. Beneath the blazing sun, the whole plain soon became a steaming, luxuriant sea of green.

But in icy February everyone was still wrapped in skin-lined or wadded cotton gowns and trousers bound at the ankles. Iron stoves burning the cheap local coal kept the wintry atmosphere out of the homes. Mr. Stanley Smith had left for furlough the previous year, leaving Mr. Glover, with only three years' experience in China, responsible for the station. But the work of evangelism and Bible teaching at the "True Religion of Jesus" centre was proceeding normally. Mrs. Glover necessarily remained with the children on the station, assisting Miss Gates, among the women, but Mr. Glover was frequently away from home on long evangelistic journeys. Miss Gates was an older woman with fifteen years' experience in China.

News from the outside world filtered through to this remote city only very slowly. The first time that Mr. and

Mrs. Glover ever heard of the existence of a secret society called the Boxers was during that ominous February. One day, their cook came in to ask permission to make the long journey to his home in the province of Shantung, ten days to the east. There, he said, his property was being threatened by the "Ta Tao Huei".

"And what are they?" Mr. Glover inquired.

"What! Hasn't the pastor heard of what is going on in Shantung? The 'Guild of the Great Sword' are looting the houses of the Christians, and even putting some to death."

No, Mr. Glover had never before heard of this secret society. The servant was given leave to go, but his reports were taken with a grain of salt—as one must do with the rumours which are constantly put about in China. Little did the Glovers realize how that expression "Ta Tao Huei", then heard for the first time, was to be burned into their very souls.

In Peking, the Reform party which desired a rapid westernization of China was meeting with bitter opposition. Conservative government officials, proud of China's ancient culture, prophesied no good if China were to adopt the ways of the West. Had not British merchants, under the guns of naval vessels, forced opium on the nation and brought limitless misery to the Chinese people in consequence? If that was the kind of thing that was to be expected from the West, then the less China had to do with "outside kingdoms" the better! The Empress Dowager sided with the reactionary conservatives and gave her patronage to the patriotic but fanatical secret society known as the "Ta Tao Huei" or "I Ho Chuan"

(Boxers). These people were bitterly anti-foreign and equally violently anti-Christian, determined to wipe out the Christian Church in China. Their headquarters were at first in Shantung, their leader being the notorious Yü-hsien, later known as the "Butcher of Shansi". When he was appointed to Shansi as viceroy of that province, he transferred the headquarters of the Boxer Movement to Taiyuan, the provincial capital.

Soon after Chu-erh, the Glovers' servant, had left for Shantung, letters were received from fellow missionaries in the neighbouring province of Chihli[1] reporting the extension of Boxer activities to their vicinity. One sentence in these letters sent a cold shudder of foreboding down their spines: "Who can tell whereunto this will grow?" The presentiment that they too might soon be involved was confirmed when, while Mr. Glover with Dr. Julius Hewitt, from a neighbouring mission station, was on an itineration to the south of Luan, voices in the crowd at an open-air meeting called out, "You foreigners won't be here long! The 'Ta Tao Huei' are going to kill you all. Look out!"

Spring arrived. Wadded winter clothing was packed away. But the skies remained a cloudless blue. The rains upon which the wheat harvest depended did not come. The green shoots were shrivelling up in the ground for want of moisture. The long continuing drought threatened a serious famine. For several years in succession, the harvest had been going from bad to worse and, even in the previous year, the distress of the people of Luan had been so great that it all but culminated in a riot in the summer.

[1] Chihli was the old name for the province better known as Hopeh.

The mission premises and even the lives of the missionaries had been threatened. The customary rain procession to propitiate the gods went past the main entrance of the missionary residence. Thousands of people took part, led by a group of men beating out a wild, exciting rhythm on drums and gongs. They had the worst intentions.

But as the missionaries made earnest prayer to God, the chief official in the city, the Prefect, unknown to the missionaries, stationed a guard of soldiers at the gates, while he himself and several of the leading gentry stood by to keep the rioters in check. That was in 1899. For yet another year, April and May had passed with nothing more than a bare sprinkling from a shower or two, which only seemed to mock the hopes of the people. What they needed was a rain to soak the ground to a depth of six inches—a "deep downpour" as they call it. The export of grain from the district was forbidden on penalty of a severe flogging and a heavy fine. The Prefect himself made special pilgrimages to the city temple to entreat the favour of Heaven. And the first week in June was fixed for a series of rain-processions through the streets and fields.

In times of public calamity, the superstitious mind of the heathen casts about in every direction for the cause; and the Chinese used invariably to find a scapegoat in the hated foreigner. Rumours were put about that the foreigner had poisoned the wells and this report was widely believed. Consequently, the attitude of the people changed. Outward friendliness changed to indifference and indifference to unconcealed aversion and open contempt.

B

The hissed "yang kuei-tzu!" ("foreign devil") as the missionaries passed along the road became the rule rather than the exception. Women, once friendly, were fearful to have any contact with the women missionaries, Mrs. Glover and Miss Gates, and attendance at the Sunday services and at open-air meetings dwindled to nothing; The priest declared, "The foreigner has blasphemed our gods in proclaiming them to be no gods; and he has insulted their majesty by bringing in his own gods; so foreign blood must be spilt before we have rain!"

The state of popular feeling in the early summer of 1900 was thus ripe for any organized development of lawlessness and it was taken full advantage of by the initiators of the Imperial Boxer Movement. This movement had the official support of the three great Chinese religions— Buddhism, Taoism and Confucianism. The Pope of the Taoist religion, in an interview with the Empress Dowager, had even counselled the slaughter of the foreigner. Yü-hsien had been installed as viceroy of Shansi on April 18th and had already been doing his utmost to foster the Boxer movement in the province. His emissaries were everywhere in evidence, recruiting in city, town and village; and the recruits were being drilled in broad daylight. Earlier in May, a murderous assault had been made on an elder of the Hungtung church, founded by the beloved Pastor Hsi. Mr. William Cooper, the superintendent of the province, felt this to be an earnest of what the Church in every part of Shansi might at any time be subjected to and in all his pastoral travels the burden of his message to the Christians was that they should prepare for persecution. Mr. Cooper passed through Luan at the end of May after visiting Hungtung and on his way to Tientsin and Shanghai, via Shunteh and Paoting in the province of Chihli. Mr. Glover escorted him the fifteen miles to Lucheng where, on June 4th, they parted with a last greeting, "The Lord be with you!"

Mr. Glover returned to Luan to find that the rain processions had already begun. Such times were always fraught with a peculiar element of danger and every rainless day made the missionaries' situation more critical. News of the official encouragement given to the Boxer movement was spreading fast and the people were becoming bolder in their hostility. The missionaries committed themselves to the Lord's protection, but entertained no thought of leaving their post, believing that the same Lord who had so wonderfully interposed for their protection the previous year would do so again if the need arose.

"The following night, June 5th," Mr. Glover wrote, "between 12 and 1 o'clock a.m. we were roused by the noise of a rain procession nearing the premises on the main north street. We held our breath as we heard the sounding gong and the thump of the drum beating out its monotonous measure. They halted opposite us. Then cries and curses were heard, soon there was battering at the gate; stones and brick-bats were flung over the wall and the gate house into the courtyard where our own quarters were. Hurriedly we got up, every moment expecting the gate to be broken in. As we were about to take the children from their beds, the volleying and battering ceased, the procession resumed its march and the terrifying noise of curses, gongs and drums died away, only to be renewed by the south quarter of the buildings where our native helpers were sleeping. Despite a prolonged attack, as though restrained once more in their attempts by some unseen hand, they again withdrew, shouting threats of revenge should the drought continue. Again with a deep sense of thankfulness we committed ourselves to our Father's protection and lay down."

Mr. Glover was faced with a terrible decision. He had two children of four and three to consider. His wife was within three months of her confinement. To remain in Luan would entail a period of severe nervous tension and great physical danger. The alternative was to take her and the children at once to the coast before the weather became too hot to travel. But it would seem wrong to forsake the Christians in the hour of their trial and there was also Miss Gates to consider. Yet it was insistently borne in on Mr. Glover that it was right to take his family to a place of safety. So Mr. and Mrs. Glover confided in their fellow workers and they all joined in prayer that the Lord would confirm this guidance in some way. The confirmation came in the willingness of the evangelist Mr. Wang and Mrs. Glover's helper Mrs. Chang to make the journey to the coast with the family. Miss Gates, however, could not be persuaded to leave the station. Her willingness to face whatever was to come was a conspicuous instance of courage and fidelity.

"It was a deep trial to be leaving the little church," said Mr. Glover, "even though it were only for a few months, in view of the prospect of famine and even, it might be, of persecution. There was also the pain of leaving behind our sister and valued helper, knowing as we did the loneliness of the path she was taking. Our hearts were heavy indeed as we made preparations to leave. I well remember my message to the brethren as we met for worship for the last time before our departure: 'Let not your heart be troubled; ye believe in God, believe also in Me.' It was the word of the Lord to my own soul first and a source of comfort to many in the days ahead."

Later in the month, on June 25th, a proclamation, evidently the substance of the Imperial Decrees of the 21st of that month, was posted up at the telegraph office at Taiyuan, the new headquarters of the Boxers. The concluding words, addressed to Chinese Christian converts, were: "Foreign religions are reckless and oppressive, disrespectful to the gods and oppressive to the people. The 'Righteous People' (viz. the Boxers) will burn and kill. Your judgments from Heaven are about to come. Turn from the false and revert to the true. Is it not benevolence to exhort you people of the Christian religion? Therefore be quick and reform. If you do your duty, you are good people. If you do not repent, there will be no opportunity for second thoughts. For this purpose is this proclamation put forth. Let all comply with it."

Before the end of the year, thousands of Chinese believers, refusing to deny their Lord, had sealed their testimony with their blood. The dreadful Boxer Year, naturally associated in the minds of Western readers with the massacre of foreign missionaries, was for the infant Chinese Church its baptism of fire.

CHAPTER ONE

THE RUMBLINGS OF THE STORM

BY the morning of Saturday, June 9th, everything was ready for the start. In order to keep the fact of our departure as far as possible from the notice of the city people, we decided to ride our own animals as far as Lucheng and hire the necessary mule litters from there. We started at ten o'clock, having sent on the baggage to avoid attracting attention. My wife and I each rode a donkey, while Hedley and Hope travelled in the cart with Mrs. Chang. It took just five hours to cover the fifteen miles and five hours in the saddle under a hot sun was very exhausting to one in my wife's condition. We had decided to complete the whole journey without dismounting in order to prevent curiosity and talk. So that when we arrived about four o'clock she was very, very weary. What a loving welcome awaited us from Mr. and Mrs. E. J. Cooper, whom my wife now met for the first time. The Sunday was spent quietly in Lucheng with Mr. and Mrs. Cooper and their two children, Edith aged five and Brainerd aged two.

The mules, together with the mule litter, were ready to start about eight o'clock on Monday morning. This mode of travel can be reasonably comfortable: between two long poles an open-meshed net is firmly secured. The baggage is then arranged in the net and covered over with softer articles such as the bedding necessary for overnight stays in the inns. As protection from the heat and glare of the sun, a woven straw mat is secured to the poles, forming a circular canopy which completely hides the occupants who are reclining inside. The whole thing is lifted on to the backs of two mules, one in front and one behind. On this occasion we took the precaution of fixing a curtain in front of the opening to be let down whenever it seemed expedient to hide the identity of the occupants. By half-past ten all were as snug as possible and ready for the road.

Before we left, further news reached us of the activities and the threats of the Boxers in the province and it was evident that the situation was becoming extremely critical. This gave a particular poignancy to the farewell to the Lucheng missionaries, four of whom were shortly to be martyred. We said goodbye, the litters were hoisted to the mules' backs and we were off. My wife and Hope led the way in the first litter, followed by Mrs. Chang riding a pack mule; I came next in the second litter with Hedley, with Chi-fah bringing up the rear on a donkey.

The full details of the journeyings on which our little family had now embarked can never be adequately described. From the day that we left our own station on June 9th to the day that we reached a safe destination in Hankow on August 14th there were sixty-seven days, during which we covered just over one thousand English miles. The period includes the season of "great heat" and the summer of 1900 proved to be the hottest for thirty years. Under the most favourable conditions, the journey would have been arduous in the extreme, but under the circumstances to be described it is indeed a miracle that any of the party survived at all.

Our litters had been hired to Shunteh in the neighbouring province of Chihli. From there we intended hiring again to Paoting. The real difficulties of the journey would then be over, and the rest of the way could be completed by river to Tientsin. This was the route which Mr. William Cooper was taking and he was only a week in advance of us. More than once we regretted that we were not travelling with him, but it was in the mercy of God that we were not, as things turned out.

All was quiet as we travelled through the pleasing, fresh countryside to Licheng, the next city of any size, where we were to sleep the first night. We had no occasion to lower the curtains. Probably this was due to the fact that rain sufficient for the present need had fallen in the neighbourhood and allayed for a time the excitable tendencies of the people. Most of them were busy in the fields with no leisure to be engaged in mischief. For this we thanked God and took courage. It seemed as though we might get through without trouble.

After a night at Licheng, the muleteers disobeyed my orders and turned off the high road to follow a "small" road on which there was less traffic. But the track lay over the roughest, wildest path through the heart of the Taihang mountains. More than once the muleteers lost their way and took us into trackless, ugly places whose solitude and desolation were forbidding. The mules—old and broken-kneed, unfortunately for us—were continually stumbling over the rocky steeps and in the torrent beds. This had the double effect of imparting a distressing pitch to the litter and giving the sensation of seasickness and of keeping the nerves perpetually on the stretch for fear of a spill. Often in going down or up the rocky passes the only way the animals could keep their feet on the slippery stones was by planting them in holes worn by the immemorial traffic. It was not long before the stumbling turned to tumbling. The front animal of the litter that was carrying my wife fell, pitching her violently forward, while the hind mule was doing his restive best to work out from under the poles. I had to witness from a distance the struggles of the beast to get up under the driver's lash and the terrible jerk of the last vigorous effort that set him on his feet again. This caused me great concern and anxiety on my wife's account. I tried exchanging litters, hoping that as my animals had not yet fallen, they had something to recommend them over others. But soon we were both down and that illusion was dispelled.

Added to this was the fact that the inns on this lesser road were only suitable for muleteers and never intended for passengers; the rooms were of the filthiest and the food of the coarsest. Thus the quiet restful sleep, so essential for my wife, after the fatigues of a long day's journey in the heat, was denied: the tiny, grimy rooms were too stifling and the vermin too lively to permit such a thing. The nights were, for her, torture and the children became so bug-bitten about the face that people wondered if they were not suffering from smallpox.

Thus the waywardness of the muleteers in bringing us by this route only increased the discomforts and weariness of the journey. Moreover, on this less frequented route, we were naturally the objects of special curiosity. Our halts for meals and at night were therefore times of real apprehension for us. In the ordinary way we thought little of curious crowds. But the circumstances under which we were travelling were out of the ordinary. The muleteers hinted at this when I repeatedly remonstrated with them for bringing us by such a dreadful road. They only replied that they had done so purposely in order to avoid publicity, for the rumours about the "foreign devil" were so evil and the temper of the people so inflammatory by reason of the drought, that it would have been highly dangerous to take the main road. This was not reassuring. We feared that even these people off the beaten track might not be entirely unaware of the current rumours nor unaffected by the prevalent exasperation caused by the drought. We could never be sure that their curiosity might not turn into hostility. It was always a relief to be back in our litters after a stop and on the move again without having encountered an angry demonstration.

The third day we found that our fears were not groundless. At noon we halted in a village too insignificant to boast an inn. The litters were therefore set down in the narrow street and we were told to make our way to the food shop which had a so-called "guest room" opening out of it. Here we undid our food box and began to prepare the children's meal. Before it was ready, the yard was thronged and the room itself packed with a gaping crowd. The heat was great and the atmosphere of the room soon became overpowering. We answered the questions that were put to us politely and pleasantly as we went on with our meal. But the crowds continued to press in upon us until my wife became faint and sick. Eating became a difficulty and rest was out of the question. Finally, Chi-fah, by appealing to their better feelings, persuaded the people in the room to leave and then tried to secure the boltless door. But in vain, for the door was then lifted from its hinges and the crowd swarmed in more boisterous than ever.

Seeing the temper of the crowd, the proprietor now sent us word to go and Chi-fah told us that we must leave without delay. So we were forced out to our litters to snatch what food we could sitting in the broiling sun amid a rude, menacing mob. We were a full two hours waiting for the head muleteer who was an opium sot and therefore immovable until he had had his fill of the drug. At last the men appeared leading out the animals and it was with profound relief that we passed out of the village gate leaving the crowd behind.

As we proceeded, we found it advisable to stop only when absolutely necessary and to make our stops shorter and our morning starts earlier. On Friday, June 14th, we reached our last halt for the midday meal before Shunteh. The prospect of being with friends again the same evening and in the comfort of a home was never so delightful as now. We entered the private home where we were to rest with thanksgiving to God and in good spirits. Our hostess received us with courtesy and an unusual show of friendliness. Food was brought in and we were just giving thanks when a man came in and entered into conversation with Chi-fah. As they sat squatting by the door and talking, food bowls in hand, I noticed their voices sink to a low undertone and I saw Chi-fah's face change colour. Involuntarily he set the bowl down and listened intently to what the man was saying.

"What is it, Chi-fah?" I asked. "Is there anything wrong?"

"God help us now, Pastor!" he replied. "Shunteh is in an uproar. The sub-Prefect's yamen has been burned, the Roman Catholic premises destroyed and there is not a single foreigner left in the city. All have fled!"

That was a dreadful moment. It seemed as if I had suddenly stepped out of bright sunshine into darkness. My wife had lain down to rest on the kang[1] but she guessed that something was amiss. The information received, far from causing alarm to her, was but the signal for her faith to take fresh hold of God. What could we do? Where could we go? Before us, it seemed, was riot and certain destruction; behind us, if we turned back, six days of difficulties such as we had just experienced. As we knelt with Chi-fah in prayer for strength and guidance, the peace of God flowed like a river. The conviction came that we should go forward. There was at least the chance that the report might be exaggerated and the China Inland Mission station unaffected. The first thing to do, therefore, was to find out whether, in fact, there were any missionaries still in the city. If not we would place ourselves directly under the protection of the Prefect, for Shunteh was a prefectural city. Our informant, a Roman Catholic, agreed, for a remuneration, to try to take a letter to Mr. Martin Griffith, the missionary in charge of the China Inland Mission station. We planned to follow later and arranged with the man to await us at a certain place on the road.

[1] The sleeping platform built of bricks and heated by a flue from a stove. It varies in size: the small single kang, the family size kang or the size found in inns accommodating many sleepers.

It was then about 2 p.m. Our decision to delay our departure was to give the messenger time to deliver the message and return and to avoid arriving ourselves at the city gates before dark. Meanwhile our hostess continued to show us great kindness and my wife was encouraged to speak freely to her the Word of Life. What was our distress when she suddenly became demon-possessed—a most distressing sight to witness. There was no violence of any kind. She simply sat on her doorstep looking straight before her, with dulled eyes, dead to all expression and apparently just going off into a swoon. Later she began an incantation, the weird strain of which made one's flesh creep. The atmosphere about us seemed suddenly impregnated with a subtle influence of evil unknown before. We discovered that this woman was a witch or medium and was in consequence subject to such possession at any time. The danger we had to fear was that the bystanders would lay this devil possession at our door and say that it was the result of the presence of "foreign devils".

Chi-fah therefore decided that we must resume our journey immediately and get away from the place. As we moved down the street we could still hear the rise and fall of the witch's chant, fainter and fainter until we were out of earshot. There was nothing said or done to us as the cavalcade proceeded towards the village gate. Doubtless the people were thankful to see the last of us. Had we tarried, they might have taken matters into their own hands to get rid of us.

Full of anxious thoughts, we progressed towards Shunteh, expecting at any moment to meet the messenger bringing us authentic news. On and on we went, but without any sign of the letter bearer. The suspense was almost unbearable. At last my curtain was pulled aside. It was Chi-fah.

"What are the Pastor's instructions now?" he whispered. "We have passed the appointed place and the man has missed us."

"Tell the muleteers to drive us right into the Prefect's yamen!" was the only possible answer.

It was just upon eleven o'clock at night as we saw the dark line of the city wall stand out before us. The drivers proceeded even more cautiously. The bells were removed from the necks of the mules so that our entrance might be as quiet as possible. A death-like stillness reigned. Not a sound was heard except the going of the mules. As we approached the bridge leading to the city gate, my curtain was again drawn aside by Chi-fah.

"What is it? Tell me!" I said.

"Blessed be God," he replied, "Mr. Griffith is in the city and has sent his servant here to await our arrival. He himself has gone to the other gate to meet you, in case you should have been entering the city that way."

The tension of eight hours could find relief only in tears. There was the man standing, lantern in hand, and he appeared in my eyes as an angel of God. I looked up, and there was my dear wife's litter standing close to mine.

"Oh, Archie!" she said, "isn't it too wonderful! God has heard our cry!"

Though it was eleven o'clock, strange to say the gate was open and we could enter unnoticed. As I sat behind the curtains and listened, not a sound save the noise of the mules' hoofs broke the stillness. The city was wrapped in sleep. Almost before we were aware of it the litters had stopped, lanterns were lifted and the faces of the dear friends we had scarcely hoped to see were looking in upon us, with words of loving greeting in whispers on their lips.

CHAPTER TWO

THE STORM BREAKS

IT was not long before we were in possession of the real facts. The messenger had faithfully fulfilled his trust and delivered the letter to Mr. Griffith. Why he failed to meet us on the road we never knew. But the object had been achieved. Our friends, who had not fled, were warned of our coming and prepared a welcome.

The report about events in Shunteh which had so alarmed us proved to have been exaggerated. While there had been incidents in connection with the Roman Catholics and with the sub-Prefect's yamen,[1] there had been no actual riot and the foreigners had not left the city. Roman Catholicism, incidentally, was one of the contributing factors to the Boxer Rising. Foreign priests openly engaged in political intrigue and interfered in the law-courts on behalf of their own adherents. Their arrogant attitude towards the Chinese authorities and their unscrupulous methods of work had brought down upon the Catholic Church the bitter hatred of the people.

The state of popular feeling following the incidents mentioned was highly inflammatory and it was generally believed that not a foreigner remained. It was therefore a remarkable providence that we had entered the city when we did and not earlier when a large, idolatrous fair was

---

[1] Offices of local government—equivalent to "town hall".

in full swing. It was also remarkable that the streets were so deserted when we arrived, whereas, on the previous night, the revelry had continued until after midnight. As it was, our coming was a dead secret to the city and Mr. Griffith begged us to keep out of sight and not to attempt to show ourselves even at the front gate. So for the eleven happy days of our stay in Shunteh, we remained within the mission premises. This precaution proved to be only too necessary.

Those days at Shunteh were unspeakably precious to us. Our friends there never revealed the fact that they were risking their lives to shelter us. If once the secret of our arrival had leaked out, their peril would have been very great. It was, in fact, our coming that eventually caused the riot in which they lost everything and which compelled them to face what seemed to be certain death in flight.

Meanwhile, as we gathered something of the extent of the Boxer Rising, it became clear that we must abandon, or at least defer, any hopes of continuing our journey towards the coast. We were deeply anxious about the safety of Mr. William Cooper who had left Shunteh for Paoting that very week. A telegram from Shanghai urging his return south through Honan province arrived too late, but was the means of leading me, later on, to seek escape in that direction. I studied the route while at Shunteh and knew how to act when the emergency arose.

All postal communication had already been disrupted and no reply was received to a letter asking for advice from Paoting. Mr. William Cooper's servant, however, called at Shunteh on his return from Paoting and reported the serious dangers of that route. This report led Chi-fah and Mrs. Chang to tell us that, if we decided to go on, they did not feel that they could accompany us any further. We realized, of course, that to go on without trustworthy Chinese to escort us would be madness. To remove any lingering thoughts of trying to go forward to the coast, news of the gravest kind reached us from the city of Hwailu, lying between Shunteh and Paoting and a C.I.M. centre of missionary work. Mr. C. H. S. Green reported the murder of a large party, including several ladies, who had tried to escape from Paoting to Tientsin. All these reports taken together showed us that the only path now open to us was to return to Luan. The decision was clinched when it became known at last that "foreign devils" were still in the house. The rumours became so ugly that the landlord insisted on our leaving before the mob pulled the house down about our ears.

On June 26th, therefore, litters were engaged for the return journey to Luan. It was not a moment too soon. Even as we were making ready the crowd were battering at the doors. They were only restrained from an attack on us by the visible evidence afforded them by the litter that we were clearing out. To our surprise and great relief, there was no demonstration as we moved along the street towards the city gate. Mr. Griffith accompanied us on foot for about a mile and then returned.

The muleteers had the strictest instructions to follow the high road in accordance with the terms written in the contract for the journey. The first day's journey took us to the muleteers' own home, where, they said, they must complete their preparations for the journey. This was in itself a deviation, and one which cost us dearly.

After spending the night at the village, we set off the next morning by the "small road". Remembering our earlier journey by this route, my heart sank, though the muleteers promised that we would rejoin the main road further on. Although we might be at the mercy of unprincipled men, we were equally certain that we were in our Father's hand. We covered the usual fifteen-mile forenoon stage without annoyance and halted for a meal at a village called Icheng. All was quiet as we entered the inn yard. But as we began to prepare the children's food in our room the yard began to fill with a pushing, curious crowd. It was useless to plead the heat of the day and the fatigue of travel. Every viewpoint was occupied. The paper was torn from the trellised window of the small guest-room and every aperture framed a face. Glass windows were of course unknown in those parts. We were fairly used to this kind of thing by now and would not have been troubled by it were it not for the uncertainty of what might be stirring in the people's minds.

We had scarcely swallowed a bowl of food when Chi-fah came in and said, "We must be off at once or I cannot answer for the consequences!" As quickly as possible, but without betraying undue haste, we settled ourselves once more in our litters, almost unfed and wholly unrested. The crowd had now grown to immense proportions. The whole of that large village seemed to be thronging around us as we went down the street. Suddenly, as we cleared the gate, a yell went up, "Foreign devils! kill them!" and a storm of stones and hard clay clods rained about the litters.

A large stone hit our little boy who was sitting on the shafts full in the chest and knocked him flat. The dear little fellow cried bitterly, but soon recovered as I told him not to be afraid because God was with us. Several stones found their way into the litter but I parried them with a pillow. The mules were hit and became very restive and it was only by shifting now to one side and now to the other that I prevented the litter from overturning.

Just as the litters seemed about to fall to pieces, the stoning all but ceased and a big powerful man seized the head of the leading mule in my team and ordered me to get out. When I demurred, he shouted:

"You are Roman Catholics! Get down, I tell you!"

Fortunately I was able to convince them that we were not Roman Catholics but Protestants, and with that the big man shouted, "Let them go on!" And suiting the action to the word he got hold of the mule's bit and forced the litter on saying, "Off with you out of this place as fast as you can! We do not want you here."

Only too thankful for this turn in events, I was just urging the muleteers on when Chi-fah rushed up, caught the animal's head and like one desperate forced him round.

"Is the Pastor talking madness?" he said. "At all costs we must return to the village."

It was only when we turned round that I saw my wife's litter in the midst of the surging crowd, battered and torn and all but a wreck. Finally the litters were driven back to the village and we were lodged in a small, dark room behind a food shop just inside the gate. Once the litters were inside the courtyard, the doors were shut on the crowd and, for several hours, there was a lull in the storm.

As we spread our bedding on the *kang*, we were able to compare notes about our recent experiences. Food was brought and after they had eaten, my wife and the children soon fell asleep. In spite of constant battering at the front gate, no one was at first allowed admittance except a handful of men. But as evening fell, a side door was opened and a continuous stream of men, women and children kept coming in and out of the room until a late hour. The heat was stifling and we were already exhausted after the strain of an anxious day. Even when the room finally cleared, we were still pelted at through the window and the curtain I put up for protection was immediately torn down.

All that night Chi-fah and Mrs. Chang sat in conclave with four or five of the people's representatives while I kept watch by the window. It was a night of alarms and fears. Every now and again Chi-fah came over to tell me the result of the negotiations. They were demanding ransom money and had decided on an impossible sum. The alternative was that we were to be handed over to the Boxers, two of whom were that night sleeping in the house. Five times at intervals during the night a gun was fired at the street door. Hands outside the window tried to push back the bundle of clothing which I had put against the window for protection and I feared that we might be shot as we lay on the *kang*. So I set my back against the bundle and gave myself to prayer while the rest of the family slept.

In the small hours, while it was yet dark, Chi-fah came to me, his haggard face looking years older, and whispered,

"The negotiations have failed. Our hope is in God alone!"

Just at that moment my wife was rousing to wakefulness and instantly guessing something was amiss asked, "What is Chi-fah saying? Tell me all." She received the news with great calmness and proposed that the four of us join together in prayer. Then we quietly discussed the situation and the suggestion made by the muleteers that we should escape under cover of darkness. However, it was clear the risk of leaving was greater than that of staying. We therefore decided that, if we had to die, we would die where we were. The authorities would then be compelled to take cognizance of the crime. It was well that we did so decide, for we later learned that liers in wait watched all night outside the village to kill us in such a way that no one could be held responsible.

Very early, as soon as it was light, the crowds began to pour in upon us once again. They even climbed on to the *kang* to pull our belongings about and examine carefully all we had. We were clearly the objects of general contempt. At length the proprietor appeared with one or two others and in peremptory tones ordered everyone out. Immediately a dozen or so evil-looking men were admitted and they began a close and most offensive scrutiny. Chi-fah, to my dismay, was nowhere to be seen. Mrs. Chang, however, sat by my wife on the *kang* and answered the questions for her. The object of this scrutiny was to see if we had the marks on us which would identify us as devils. As they put their sinister faces close to ours and examined the colour of our eyes, my heart sickened with fear as they drew the children forward and said,

"Look at these little devils; their eyes are blue as the big ones!" It was the common belief that blue eyes were the mark of being a devil!

It now seemed evident to me that the room had been cleared and these men introduced for one purpose only. The ransom demanded was not forthcoming and the alternative was death. I saw in these men our executioners. Their awful faces were enough, but when one of them produced two steel daggers, bayonet-shaped, and began toying with them before our eyes, all doubt was gone and I could only pray God that He would now give us, each one, the special grace for such an hour. The suspense of that terrible moment was possibly the more agonizing in that it was the first of many similar situations and because the terrors of a violent death were at that time fresh to me.

The strain was relieved by the sudden appearance of Chi-fah, though his face showed no sign of hope. "We are ordered to leave," he said; "the proprietor refuses to keep us here any longer." Without further ado, the proprietor himself pushed in, snatched the coverlets from the *kang* and, cursing us as he went, carried them outside. There was nothing to do but to follow. As we marched out in single file, with the man carrying the daggers immediately behind me, we believed that it was to our death. We surmised that the proprietor, refusing to stain his hands with our blood, was handing us over to the mob. We were therefore not prepared for the astounding turn of events when we came to the street. Dense masses of people lined the roadway on either side, but our appearance was greeted, not by a rage of fury, but by a silence so profound as to be awful to the senses. It seemed impossible that it could be otherwise than ominous of ill. A narrow pathway through the crowd showed our litters set down in the road, repaired and ready packed with the mules beside them. Just beyond, on a grassy knoll, high above the crowd, stood a commanding figure in a white silk gown, motionless save for the slow flutter of his fan. It was the local mayor. I can see him now, standing like a statue with calm and dignified bearing, the centre of the whole scene. The proprietor led us straight to our litters, where several men, the elders of the village, were standing. They directed us to get in. Almost before we could settle ourselves on the bedding, we were hoisted to the mules' backs. Then, to my amazement, the mayor came down from his vantage ground, took the leading mule's bridle without a word and led my wife's litter to the village gate. Close behind him followed the village elders, one of whom led my litter in the same way. Not a soul of all that huge multitude moved from his place as we passed along the narrow lane they left for us. I thought of yesterday and how they had waited till we were outside the gate before they set on us and I fully expected that the silence and restraint would soon give way to a repetition of tumult and violence. But we passed through the gates and there was still no sound. The mayor and the elders were still leading the animals and the road behind us was deserted. In this way we were escorted to the village boundary where the mayor made us a courteous bow and returned, followed by the village elders.

It is impossible to describe the state of our feelings when we found ourselves still alive and free once more. We were

both conscious that it was nothing less than a direct intervention of God on our behalf. Songs of thanksgiving were
in our mouths as we spoke with one another from the
litters. It was only later, however, that we learned from
Chi-fah how really miraculous our escape had been.
There was nothing to account for the mayor's espousal of
our cause. That the people, robbed of their ransom money,
should have been held in as they were, unable to lift a
finger against us, was nothing but the work of God.
Again and again in subsequent experiences we were per-
mitted to see the same supernatural phenomenon; but
this first manifestation of it, though by no means the most
remarkable, left an impression peculiarly its own.

CHAPTER THREE

INTO THE VALLEY OF THE SHADOW

OUR muleteers now resumed charge of the litters and we journeyed quietly on with praiseful hearts. I longed, however, for the time when we should strike the highway, as my fears about the "small" road had already proved to be well grounded. We had gone perhaps a mile and a half when I saw a band of about twenty men spring from the roadside and make for my wife's litter, which was now about a hundred yards ahead of mine. At the same time others came running over the fields to join them. My heart sank. I called aloud upon God as I saw my wife and Hope surrounded, unprotected and out of reach of my care. I shouted for Chi-fah who should have been riding close behind me, but there was no reply. With difficulty I made a hole in the rush matting at my back and through it I saw a crowd in full pursuit, with our attendants nowhere to be seen.

My own litter was now quickly surrounded and it was evident that we were prisoners once more. They set about robbing us of anything they could lay their hands on. I was horrified to see the men in front slash the cords which held together the framework of my wife's litter and tear the matting from the poles. I could thus see her supporting little Hope with one hand and trying to protect her possessions with the other. The litter was tilted to such an impossible angle that it was a marvel how she could maintain her balance. Every moment I expected to see her roll heavily to the ground. Then she disappeared round a bend in the road and I wondered whether I should ever see her alive again. The distance between us had been increasing and when I reached the bend the party in front was nowhere to be seen. The path led down a steep incline to a dry torrent bed and while the plundering and wrecking of my litter continued I was far more concerned about my loved ones and what might have happened to them. At last we reached the foot of the slope where I caught sight of my dear wife's litter set down on the ground in the middle of the torrent bed, with both her and my little girl sitting within it. My own litter was then set down in the same way beside hers and the animals led away. To my amazement she was quite calm and free from agitation.

It was now about 9 a.m. and the sun was getting hot. The sky was cloudless. Since leaving Icheng we had seen nothing of Mrs. Chang or Chi-fah and had no idea what had become of them. We were soon hemmed in by hundreds of curious villagers who would normally have been at work in the fields but whose work had been brought to a standstill by the unbroken drought. Quiet, inoffensive labourers had been turned into potential mischief-makers by the disaster. Soon, to our great relief, for we knew not what to do, we saw our two Chinese friends making their way on foot towards us. Their animals had been taken from them. They told us that we were again to be held to ransom and that we would not be allowed to leave our present situation in the torrent bed until an earnest of the amount demanded had been paid down. For six long, weary hours, under the scorching sun and deprived of the normal shelter through the destruction of our litters, the haggling went on to decide the price to be paid. It was indeed a time of testing but we found our God again to be a very present help and our shield and strength. Grace sufficient to endure the heat and the cravings of hunger and thirst was richly supplied, as well as a forbearing spirit and courteous manner towards those who thrust themselves so rudely upon us or plied us with unending contemptuous questions. Nor was our behaviour wholly lost upon them. The heart of one old woman was so touched that she sent her son home for a kettle of boiled water for us to drink, repeating this kindness until our need was satisfied.

At last our captors decided to demand one hundred ounces of silver. This we absolutely refused. Eventually, after the prolongation of our discomfort, the amount was reduced first to fifty and finally to thirty ounces. We were to pay down ten on the spot before we moved. There was nothing to do but agree. The problem was how to get at the silver without the crowd knowing what I was doing. In the providence of God I had weighed out a number of small ingots before leaving Luan and marked each nugget with the exact weight. These I kept in a small packet under my bedding, ready at hand in case of need. Covered by Chi-fah, I managed to open the packet without being noticed and very remarkably the few nuggets that came to hand first amounted to a trifle over the sum needed. Further fumbling might well have attracted attention. The earnest money was no sooner handed over than the village headman ordered the mules to be put in and he himself took charge of my litter. We were led up the steep and stony street until we came to a large doorway. The doors swung back and we entered a spacious courtyard which betrayed at a glance that this was the house of no ordinary man. The litters were set down and we were directed into an inner courtyard, the doors of which were promptly closed behind us. An old lady, who afterwards proved to be the headman's mother, and the headman's wife received us with a show of cordiality which was cheering as it was surprising. They showed us into a small but comfortable dwelling room and told us to rest ourselves and not be 'afraid. Bowls of millet porridge and a kettle of boiling water were quickly brought in and a hand-basin for washing purposes placed at our disposal.

Though deeply thankful for the temporary privacy and quiet, the situation was nevertheless critical. In spite of the outward show of kindness, it was clear that we were still prisoners. Chi-fah concluded from the attitude of our captors that we were in real danger. There were two courses open to us: to acquaint Mr. Griffith by letter of our peril and so secure the intervention of the Prefect of Shunteh: or to apply to the magistrate of the nearby county town of Wuan for help. He was bound by Treaty rights to secure our protection. But how were we to get a letter to either of these people? Who would dare to carry a letter for a foreigner? Only Chi-fah, and he was a marked man. "We have no might, neither know we what to do, but our eyes are upon Thee!" was exactly how we felt. We had no writing paper and, if we had, to be seen writing would only have increased our danger. In the mercy of God, I found a tiny piece of crumpled paper in my pocket and, exercising great caution, I scribbled a note to Mr. Griffith, and my wife wrote to Mrs. Griffith. Then we discovered that one of the muleteers was returning to his home near to Shunteh and, for a consideration, he consented to deliver the letter. He set off about midnight, when all was quiet, with the precious message hidden in his sock.

The next day, Friday, June 29, passed quietly. We scarcely saw Chi-fah all day. He was on the look-out for a chance to send word to the Wuan magistrate about our plight. But try as he might, no such opportunity occurred until about ten o'clock at night when he came in to see us with the words "Praise the Lord!" And he went on to say how the man in whose house we were, was connected with the Wuan yamen. Opium sot and bad character that he was, he saw a chance to make a little gain out of the situation. For fifteen ounces of silver, he was to allow Chi-fah to go with his old mother, carrying my passport and visiting card. Early the next morning, before daylight, they were gone. Thus both the plans, which had seemed equally hopeless, were fulfilled.

All Saturday we waited for the outcome. We remained in complete quiet and had several opportunities of passing on the Word of Life to the members of the household, including the headman himself. His wife particularly listened with deep interest as she heard for the first time the story of the Saviour's love for her. Hour after hour passed without any word from Shunteh or Chi-fah. Chi-fah, who should have been back by the early afternoon, was not back by nightfall. Then just at midnight, there was a noise in the outer courtyard of loud and angry voices. By the light of lanterns, the old mother was led in in a state of demon possession. They took her to her room and for the rest of the night we had to listen to the weird, unearthly chant.

It was an untold relief to see Chi-fah safely back, for as our escort, anything might have happened to him. He told us how, after considerable difficulty, he had been able to see the magistrate and had been granted an escort of ten soldiers and a petty official or two to accompany us on our way. Meanwhile, as the woman chanted in the inner courtyard, the soldiers wrangled noisily about their pay in the outer court and the headman himself raged against us in a fit of uncontrollable passion, swearing that he would not let us go until we had paid him more money. Suddenly he burst into our room, quivering with rage and cursing us all at the top of his voice. The whole place seemed to be filled with the presence of the powers of darkness.

Just when matters were at their worst, a messenger from Shunteh appeared, a well-to-do business man, of good standing and repute, and one in whom Mr. Griffith placed much confidence. He immediately addressed himself to the headman, asking him how he dared to molest us, and told him that the news of his conduct had come to the ears of the Prefect. Even now there were fifty soldiers on their way to look into matters. He himself had been sent on ahead to warn him that if we were harmed in any way or if a single cash was taken from us, he would be held responsible. The effect produced was remarkable. The erstwhile terrifying bully suddenly became the fawning sycophant. He was terrified at the thought of the fifteen ounces of silver he had demanded from us and implored us not to expose him. We reassured him that the money could be regarded, in part at least, as payment for his hospitality and services in securing for us an escort from Wuan. His gratitude was profound and from that moment he was kindness itself. He quickly adjusted the difficulty with the Wuan escort and soon all was quiet save for the haunting cadence of the old witch mother's chant.

When all were asleep, the Shunteh messenger returned and handed me a pencilled note from Mr. Griffith, written at 5 a.m. on Friday:

"Your letter just received does not reassure us. We are preparing for flight ourselves and have been up all night packing, every moment expecting a riot. We deeply grieve to hear of the peril you are in, but are powerless to help you. The Prefect will do nothing for us. Our eyes are upon God alone. We intend to sleep tonight at the muleteer's home and take cart thence to Lucheng, if possible."

I turned to the messenger and said:

"This is very different from what you said just now!"

"Hush!" he said, "not a word! It is a ruse of my own to get you out of this fix. Mischief is brewing and if you do not get out now, you never will. Just keep quiet and leave everything with me."

We lay down, but could not sleep. Our hearts were filled with wonder. God was with us, mighty in working. He had verily broken the gates of brass and cut bars of iron in sunder. We thought much of the Griffiths and their danger and our hope was that we might yet meet them at Lucheng, the city through which we would pass on our way to Luan. We did not hear of them again, however, until our two months' wandering were over: meanwhile we concluded that a violent death had overtaken them.

CHAPTER FOUR

AN ANGEL OF THE LORD

THE next day was July 1st. Our litters were once more rigged up and at eight o'clock we started out again as free men and with thankful hearts. Little did we know that this was the first day of a week of constant terror and the first of a month of undreamt of sufferings. Unknown to us, it was the day on which Mr. William Cooper, Mr. and Mrs. Bagnall and their daughter Gladys were beheaded just outside the South Gate of Paoting. For us, too, it was to be a day of darkness and the shadow of death.

Expectant crowds had gathered as usual and it was not easy to face the mob again after nearly three days of privacy. But the knowledge that we were under official protection went far to allay our anxiety. The headman led my litter, accompanied by the Shunteh messenger whose air of authority seemed to carry all before him. At the village boundary they turned back after taking a courteous leave of us, and our confidence now lay in the presence of the yamen officials and soldiers.

The next day, July 2nd, an edict was to go forth from Peking ordering the expulsion of all foreigners from China and the persecution of Christians. On June 28th, an order had already been issued from the Throne to all viceroys and governors to support the Boxer Rising. It is a

D

good thing that this information was then unknown to us, for the effect of the order was to render our passports useless and to convert our rightful protectors into our persecutors and possible murderers. Our reception all along the road to Wuan was of such a kind as to show us what our fate would have been but for the escort. The news of our payment of ransom money had gone ahead of us and consequently each little village and town through which we passed was eager for a share in the spoils. The men who accosted us were generally armed and our appearance was invariably greeted with the cry, "Kill the foreign devils!" The closely drawn curtains would be torn away and, to judge from the malicious gestures of the crowd as they cursed us out of the place, it would have gone very hard with us had not God's mercy provided official protection. Even as it was, the people were barely restrained from assaulting us.

On reaching Wuan we were driven into the yamen where the Mandarin was waiting to give us audience. I followed the usher with some trepidation, as I had never before interviewed such a dignity nor seen the inside of a yamen audience chamber. Besides, my Chinese vocabulary was still small and my knowledge of yamen etiquette inadequate. However, Chi-fah was with me and passing through several dingy courtyards we came to the Mandarin's own office. The great man himself was waiting for us in full official dress and with a small retinue of city gentry. He reached out his hand in the most fatherly way and with a genial smile led me to the seat of honour on his left. Cups of tea were brought and the reassuring manner of the kindly old man scattered all my fears to the winds.

He conversed most affably with me, examined my passport and assured me that he would do all he could to get me through to my destination without further annoyance. In due course a safe conduct pass to the Mandarin of the next city of Shaehsien was made out and an escort provided.

On returning to the family, I was surprised to find my wife seated, not in the litter where I had left her, but on the ground, looking as if she had received some shock, with the children crying bitterly by her side. Evidently the mules had become restive and the litter had been overturned, throwing them all to the ground. Thank God, there were no serious injuries, but my wife had fallen heavily enough to be badly bruised. We lost no time in getting off, as delay meant increasing crowds and corresponding danger. The escort given us consisted of six sorry-looking underlings, shortly reduced to four, and these men, provided for our protection, soon became our worst enemies.

We must have been travelling for about four hours and covered twelve miles when we came to a place where the mule track led up a broad, dry river bed. The escort had by now dwindled to two and I was feeling distinctly uneasy. At a bend in the river we saw ahead a large straggling town. In no time, excited men and lads were swarming around us shouting, "Kill the foreign devils!" When it was evident that we were about to be stoned, Chi-fah stopped the litters and asked the escort to assert its authority. Only then did they produce our papers for the headman to see, with the result that we were taken to a large, newly-built inn and the crowd was shut out. The guest-room ran the whole length of the north side of the courtyard and was only partially finished. There was a good *kang*, however, at one end and we were thankful for a roof over our heads and shelter from the intense heat.

It was the old story of a ransom price with the alternative of death. The matter was discussed in cold blood in the presence of the very men charged to protect us and with their connivance. The missing members of the escort had, as we now discovered, hastened on to warn the townsmen of our approach and to plot our arrest and a share in the loot. I never saw Chi-fah in such distress of mind. Our only hope was to inform the magistrate of Shaehsien of our difficulties, but when Chi-fah tried to slip out under cover of darkness to reach the city, our guards became so nasty that he had to give up the attempt. At nightfall, we put the children to bed and were about to retire ourselves when Chi-fah informed us that there was no hope at all of our getting out alive. It was no longer just a money question, but we were being held responsible for the prolonged drought and it was commonly believed that nothing but foreign blood would bring rain! Unless God directly intervened, nothing could save us.

"But we are under official protection and when the Government has undertaken to safeguard us, what is there to fear?"

"That goes for nothing in the circumstances," Chi-fah replied, "the escort itself has betrayed us and they can easily excuse themselves to their superiors by saying that they were overpowered by numbers."

I would have preferred to keep this news from my wife, but she insisted that however grave the news she must be allowed to enjoy fellowship in prayer with me in all things. We were therefore pouring out our hearts before God, seeking grace to endure even unto death, if it was His will, when a truly marvellous thing happened. The door opened and a soldier in full uniform entered and quietly hung his coat and weapon on a hook. His handsome face and commanding manner were something out of the common and could not fail to arrest attention. But this was not enough to account for the effect his sudden appearance produced upon all. I cannot describe it. It was simply startling. He was only a non-commissioned officer sent on special service to Licheng; and he was merely putting up at the inn for the night in the ordinary course of his journey. Yet our eyes were opened to see in him none other than God's deliverer. There seemed something supernatural about his presence. Not only so, but his coming produced a corresponding fear in the hearts of our enemies. We learned afterwards that the escort were in dismay, believing that his business was in some way connected with them. And the general impression produced was that he was charged with some important commission on our behalf.

In keeping with our conviction was the remarkable fact that from the first he identified himself with us and espoused our cause. Chi-fah invited him to eat his food within the privacy of our curtained space, and he at once accepted. The picture of the two Chinese talking earnestly in whispers in the dim flicker of the oil lamp stands out vividly in my mind. As yet we knew nothing of the stranger and could gather nothing of the tenor of his conversation, yet we seemed to know intuitively that he was God's messenger and that his words were of peace and not of evil.

After the meal, the soldier withdrew and Chi-fah came to tell us all. On the strength of the belief that he was officially connected with us, the man undertook to pass us out at dawn the next morning and accompany us to Licheng. What this news meant to us cannot even be imagined. It was literally the turning of the shadow of death into the morning. It being the Lord's Day, we determined to hold Divine service before lying down to rest. In this we were joined by the two muleteers and the soldier. As Chi-fah would be better understood than me, I asked him to read and expound the Scriptures. The soldier listened with great interest to the whole proceedings and we rejoiced that the seed of eternal life was thus sown in yet another prepared heart.

The second miracle of that memorable day followed almost immediately upon the conclusion of worship. We had pleaded with our God to have mercy upon the people, not only in their deep spiritual need, but also in their temporal distress. And we asked very definitely in the hearing of all that, for the glory of His great name, He would be pleased to send rain in abundance that night, so proving that we His servants were not the cause of the drought. Scarcely had we laid ourselves down to rest when a thundercrash shook the building and the rain began to fall. It continued in a deluge all night through. When morning broke it was clear shining after rain and the song of the Lord was in our mouths. The gate of our prison-inn opened to us, as it were, of its own accord. Our heaven-sent soldier rode beside us and never left us all the way. We scarcely saw a soul all along the road to Shaehsien, for everyone had hurried out early into the fields to take advantage of the long-looked-for opportunity for putting in the seed.

On arrival at Shaehsien, I left the family at the inn under the soldier's care, while I accompanied Chi-fah to the yamen where I was determined to obtain official protection. We had to walk the whole length of the city and, although I was wearing Chinese dress and the queue, I was recognized as a foreigner and the inevitable crowd began to follow us. By the time we reached the yamen the crowd was uncomfortably large and threatening. The Mandarin's deputy received us coldly and said it was impossible for us to see the Mandarin himself. I insisted that he should hand in my card as I had urgent business. But he returned with the excuse that his Excellency was too unwell to see me. Only when I threatened to take my case to the Prefect, his superior, was I admitted to his presence. After I had explained what I wanted, he gladly endorsed my safe-conduct pass with his seal, apparently glad to get rid of us so easily.

Without any further serious difficulties, we set off on our journey again with the precious official papers. The soldier had succeeded well in protecting my wife and children from the curious crowd outside the inn while they quietly ate their meal. We pursued our journey in peace to Licheng where we took farewell of our soldier deliverer. In addition to giving him several books we also made him a present of five hundred cash—a sum utterly inadequate for his services to us; but Chi-fah, knowing his own people best, cautioned me not to give any more. The gifts were acknowledged graciously and with every appearance of sincere gratitude.

The heavy rain had calmed the minds of the people, at least for the time being, and they were too busy in the fields to pay much attention to the party of mule litters and donkeys passing along the road to Lucheng. Our hearts were full of praise to God for all that we had seen of His glory since we last travelled along this same road.

CHAPTER FIVE

"FLEE! FLEE!"

WE reached Lucheng once more about 10 a.m. on Tuesday, July 3rd. Our friends were not wholly surprised at seeing us back, and deeply thankful at seeing us at all. Local rumours had become so serious that Mr. E. J. Cooper had already appealed for protection to the city magistrate. It appeared that in Luan the situation was equally precarious and Miss Gates was evidently under a great strain.

We determined not to tarry at Lucheng, but to push on the remaining fifteen miles as quickly as possible. A lad who attached himself to us unofficially at Wuan had already gone ahead from Lucheng with a letter to Miss Gates to prepare her for our coming. This was a gracious provision of the Lord, because we could not possibly have spared Chi-fah for such an errand. We left our more foreign-looking boxes at Lucheng and dispensed with our escort so that our return to Luan might be as inconspicuous as possible. We bid farewell for the second time to our Lucheng friends, conscious that this leave-taking had a deeper significance than usual for us all. Before any of us were to meet again in four weeks' time we were all to know, as never before, what it meant to drink of His cup and to be baptized with His baptism.

The muleteers urged the animals along and we made good progress. Though the road was perfectly quiet, we took the precaution of keeping our curtains down. About three miles from Luan we passed through the village of Kuantsuen, an outstation with a chapel and a bright band of Christians and inquirers. We saw several of these and could not forbear to peep through the curtains and exchange the Christian salutation "Peace!" though we dared not stay for more than a passing word. An hour later we were entering, for the last time, the north gate of the city. All was quiet. It was intensely hot and no one was about. The drivers were not once challenged by a passer-by. Yes, we had succeeded in entering unobserved. We soon turned the corner into the side street where our more private entrance was and a minute or two later our litters were standing within our own loved home.

The reunion with our sister, Miss Gates, was an intense relief to us all. Her path, no less than ours, had been increasingly difficult and perilous. Boxer corps had already been organized in the district and they were expected in Luan any day to carry out their dread tasks. The series of rain processions had culminated on July 1st in a grand function attended by all the senior officials in the city. When, on July 2nd, the rumours that the Empress Dowager had issued secret orders for the extermination of the foreigner became current, Miss Gates had sent all the Chinese on the compound home and made preparations to escape to the hills. The faithful Sheng-min and Pao-erh, however, refused to leave her and undertook to escort her to a mountain cave known to them and to care for her there. This was the situation on our return. We were clearly facing a crisis of the greatest gravity. We therefore united in earnest prayer for the clear knowledge of God's will.

A mysterious inquiry from the Mandarin on July 4th as to whether we were planning to go south may well have been a hint to us to make good our escape while we might, as he must have just received the edict issued that very day. The same day we heard that the missionaries at Pingyao, to the north-west, had barely escaped death from rioters and were fleeing to Lucheng where they were hourly expected. It seemed clear that similar trouble would sooner or later overtake us too. Ought we not, therefore, to be ready for flight in case of sudden emergency? The climax was reached when we learned for certain that the imperial edict calling for the destruction of all foreigners had been posted up outside the yamen and that our death was now a public topic of conversation. Indeed we heard that the actual day for our execution had been fixed for the tenth day of the sixth moon!

There was a small door in the north wall of the mission compound opening on to fields and therefore seldom unlocked. To slip out by this door to the yamen was my only hope of getting there safely. So Sheng-min and I stole out by dark and made our way through the fields to see the Mandarin. The deputy refused to admit us to his senior but offered to take a message. We sat down together and I asked about the rumours we had heard. He admitted knowing about them but made light of them and sent us back home with the words, "There is nothing to be afraid of!" My first reaction was to accept this as guidance not to leave the station. But when I awoke the next morning, July 5th, and opened my Bible at the portion for the day, it was the eighth chapter of Joshua. I came to the fifth verse, "It shall come to pass when they come out against us . . . we will flee before them." My thought was arrested and as I prayed over the passage, I heard but one voice, "Flee before them, flee before them!" I shrank from the idea after all we had just gone through. Was it possible that God was calling us to pass that way again? Then the words in verses 1 and 8 lighted up, "Fear not, neither be thou dismayed. See, I have commanded you." The call was so clear and emphatic that I felt convinced that flight was now for us a God-appointed duty. After breakfast we gathered according to our regular custom for family prayer, Miss Gates uniting, as usual, with us. We were reading consecutively through the books of Samuel and the chapter for that particular morning was 2 Samuel 15. Imagine how I felt when I came to verse 14, "And David said unto all his servants that were with him at Jerusalem, Arise and let us flee; for we shall not else escape from Absalom: make speed to depart." It was enough. Closing the book, I said, "This is the Lord's word to us. The path is clear beyond the shadow of a doubt. We have nothing to do but to obey and flee." I then told the others about my reading before breakfast and they were just as impressed as I was with this striking confirmation and recognized it as the declaration of God's will for us. We therefore set about immediately to prepare for flight.

Not long after, the Mandarin sent us a message which confirmed the truth of the rumours and informed us that he must now withdraw from us his protection. We could do as we chose, stay or go, but he was powerless to help us. This finally settled the matter. As I considered in which direction to flee I recalled the telegram from Shanghai which had arrived at Shunteh too late to prevent Mr. William Cooper from continuing in the direction of Peking. By travelling south, we believed that there were real hopes that we might soon get away from the disaffected area and reach a place of safety. We decided to hire mule litters to Chowkiachow in Honan where the China Inland Mission had a station and from there we could, if necessary, travel on to Shanghai by boat. We were not to know that Honan, too, was just as much affected as Shansi. As it was, God used our ignorance to foster hope in the days to come and to accomplish His purpose in our escape from the city.

Sheng-min accordingly was sent to secure three litters. Quietly, busily, prayerfully, the day was spent in packing, arranging the affairs of the church and distributing our belongings. We did this in order to ensure the least possible loss from the inevitable looting which would follow our departure. One of the last things I did was to send our dining-room clock as a present to the Mandarin in the hope that this might move his heart to some degree of pity for us.

Our saddest moments were when we took leave of the few Christians who came in to see us in the course of the day, for we all believed that we should never see one another's face again. Elder Liu entreated us with tears to lose no time, for to delay another day might mean certain death. The last prayers were breathed, the last exhortations and promises from the Word of God given, the last affectionate assurances exchanged and we parted.

Sheng-min came back during the noon meal to say that he had been to every place he knew in the city where carts and litters were hired, but no one was willing to take "foreign devils". What was to be done now? We were beginning to realize that in very deed we were as the filth of the world. There was a universal feeling towards us which foreboded nothing but death. I saw that, as the road to the south was our only hope, no effort must be spared to secure conveyances of some kind. So I again sent the boy out to have another try while we prayed. Oh, how earnestly we prayed! Everything hung upon the success or failure of the errand. At sunset the boy came back to say that, after hours of wearying search, and just as he was giving it up as hopeless, he happened to meet two muleteers in the west suburb. They were Roman Catholics and willing to make a secret agreement to take us to Chowkiachow for 80,000 cash.[1] The sum was exorbitant but we had no choice except to agree. There was a final threat to our plans when one of our former servants came to tell us that an order had been issued to close the city gates. He urged us to escape now on foot without our belongings and he would lower us over the city wall not far from us. But we believe that God who had given us the litters would work for us to open the gates.

[1] The ancient Chinese copper coins with a hole in the middle, making it possible to thread the coins on a string for convenience.

CHAPTER SIX

SENTENCE OF DEATH

IT was nearly midnight when the litters appeared. We had planned for the muleteers to spend the night in our own stables, so that an early start might be made with all possible secrecy. We had expected them much earlier in the evening and had begun to wonder whether the men had thought better of the bargain. It was with great relief, therefore, that we heard the clatter of hoofs upon the stones, and knew that God had provided us with the means of escape.

Though sorrow at leaving our happy life at Luan filled our hearts, the peace of God was there too. We were all wonderfully sustained for the fatigue of that busy night of preparation. In sweet unconsciousness, the two children lay asleep on the bare bed, ready dressed for the moment of flight. By lantern light we packed the three litters. It seemed like a dream. Only just off the road, and now, could it be that we were really taking the road again? While the muleteers gave the finishing touches to the litters, we knelt for the last time in our home beside the sleeping children and commended ourselves and the Christians we were leaving behind into the hands of the Heavenly Father. Then, after locking the doors behind us, we carried the children out to the litters, took our seats and were hoisted once more to the mules' backs.

The first streaks of dawn were breaking over the hills

as the little cavalcade moved off. Like a light from heaven, the promise was flashed into my dear wife's heart, "I shall not die, but live, and declare the works of the Lord." How often was this promise to carry her through the valley of death in the days to come!

Silently we stole out by the main entrance into the north street. Sheng-min accompanied us, leading our donkey. Pao-erh closed the gate after us from inside so that our flight might be unnoticed and then climbed out over the wall and caught us up. Our faithful dog "Bobs" also elected to follow us. With an almost human instinct, he seemed to guess that we would never return. The dead stillness of the sleeping city intensified the strain. We had already taken the precaution of removing the bells from the mules' necks, but even so, to my anxious ears, the ring of their hoofs upon the stones had a sound about it so loud and penetrating that one felt it could hardly fail to arouse the curious from their beds.

At length we arrived at the great south gate and halted before the massive barrier, fast closed against us. Loud and long the drivers knocked at the gate-keeper's door. In vain; not a sound from within! The light was broadening in the east and ere long men would be astir and the precious moments upon which our hope of getting outside the city hung, were swiftly passing.

Then a loud, uncouth voice, demanding who we were and what we wanted at that time of day; and—an insolent refusal to open the gate! What happened then I could not tell from inside the litter. There was silence for a time; then voices in hot debate, and then—were my ears deceived?—the creaking of the huge iron-plated leaves as they swung slowly, slowly open! Then the drivers' call to the animals and a moment later we were outside the city!

God had wrought for us very signally. For, while we had to pay a comparatively trifling sum, it was nothing short of a miracle that the man should agree to receive money at all in the circumstances. We gave God praise as we hurried on through the narrow suburb into the open country. It was now broad daylight and I began to breathe freely as the distance from the city increased without our being challenged. At the pace we were travelling we had hopes of reaching Kaoping, forty miles distant, before halting for the night. We also hoped and prayed that our flight would not soon be discovered.

We had covered about three miles when I discovered that Miss Gates' litter, which should have been following close behind mine, was nowhere to be seen. Thinking that our two litters had outpaced hers, I called a halt to give her time to catch up with us. The enforced delay was sorely trying, as every moment was of consequence. After waiting some minutes, I was just about to turn my litter back to look for the missing litter when Pao-erh came running up to report. He said that, just after clearing the suburb, a small band of men had given chase, held up the litter and demanded money before they would let her go on. She was now free and on her way again, but the discovery of our flight must have greatly lessened our chances of escape.

Miss Gates, with her fifteen years in China, was a fluent Chinese speaker and thoroughly understood all that was being said around. On rejoining us, she urged us to hurry on as quickly as possible. It was evident that

E

there was danger of being beset by one band of robbers after another from the city. Our children were by now awake and it was hard to silence the gleeful laugh and childish prattle that might betray us. They could not understand why they could not "draw the blinds" now that it was no longer night-time. But, cooped up and cramped as they were for space, and able to see nothing, their absolute obedience was beyond praise. Indeed, so far from being a trouble, the presence of our little ones throughout our flight was the greatest cheer and comfort to us, but for the corresponding sorrow that they must be exposed to such suffering.

We must have been pushing on steadily for close upon another hour, when we found ourselves suddenly pulled up. The noise of men pursuing told its own story. The fact of our flight was out. Throughout the next hour or two, we were handing out sums of money of varying amounts to satisfy the insolent demands of these robbers. If there was any demur, we were detained until the demand was complied with. No actual violence was offered us at this time, because the men were taken up for the time being with the contents of the cash bag. Not until this store was exhausted did they turn their thoughts to other things.

It was about nine o'clock when we reached the market town of Hantien. To our surprise, instead of passing on straight through the town, we were driven into the inn yard, the mules were stabled and we were shown to a room on the east side of the courtyard. Our muleteers, we discovered, had played us false and we were the victims of treachery. They had been in collusion with the robbers by the way and had now betrayed us into the hands of our enemies. From that hour for forty days to come we were to know little rest day or night, and were never free from storm and tempest and the shadow of death.

We took from our litters only those things we might need for a short halt, expecting to resume our journey an hour or so later. But any such hope was soon dispelled. The courtyard was fast filling with men; and, from the tenor of their talk and general demeanour, our two Chinese companions gathered at once that mischief was determined. Under pretext, therefore, of fetching our pillows and coverlets for a siesta, they contrived to bring in all the silver we had with us—one hundred and forty-eight ounces. Dividing the ingots amongst us, we succeeded in secreting them upon our persons without being observed.

Meanwhile, the news that the "foreign devils" were in the town had spread far and wide and the inn was soon besieged. All day long they poured in from the surrounding hamlets. Foremost amongst them all, in the bitterness of hate, were the people of Sutien and with their arrival, in the early afternoon, the situation began to take on a darker hue. Up till then I had been able to show myself in the courtyard without being molested, but now this was no longer possible. We realized that, to all intents and purposes, we were no longer guests but prisoners. The landlord treated us with marked incivility and we had the gravest difficulty in getting food. Though we had been travelling since dawn we were allowed to taste nothing till noon and absolutely nothing again. After that single meal not another morsel of food passed our lips for two days and nights.

As the day wore on the noise outside increased. Sheng-min and Pao-erh mingled with the crowd to glean all they could of their intentions. We were being held, it seemed, in revenge for the drought and as compensation for the loss of their harvest. The Sutien folk were not long in getting to business. They first stoned our faithful "Bobs" to death and killed our donkey. Then they turned their attention to our litters in a search for silver. Seeing that it was no longer safe to conceal money on our persons, we transferred it to the bed where we were sitting and hid it as best we could among the bedding.

Meanwhile, a detachment of Boxers had arrived at the inn and were discussing the situation with the leading men of the villages represented. They decided that we were to pay 200 ounces of silver as compensation for losses sustained through the drought, or be put to death. When Sheng-min came in to break the news, we saw that he was much agitated. Seating himself on the bed, he said, "The Boxers are here and we are all to be killed." Then, burying his face in his hands, he leaned his head on Miss Gates' shoulder and wept. We were all deeply affected—the more, that the children had understood and were also crying bitterly as they clung to us, questioning, "Oh, Father! Mother! what are they going to do to us? are they going to kill us? Really kill us?"

What else should we do at such a time but draw near to God? Humbly and trustfully we lifted our eyes to Him from whom alone our help could come; and as we looked at the things not seen, and yielded ourselves into His hand for life or death in the prayer that He might be glorified, the peace of God took possession of our hearts and stilled every fear. Even the children's terror was hushed to rest as they repeated after their mother, "I will trust and not be afraid!" Soon after, they were wrapped in a calm, untroubled sleep.

We now urged Sheng-min and Pao-erh to leave us and to save their own lives while they might. They both refused, knowing full well that their identification with us would almost certainly involve them in the same fate. Those dear lads literally laid down their lives for our sakes, in a surrender as disinterested as it was voluntary and deliberate. They had scarcely gone out to resume their watch in the courtyard, when suddenly the air was filled with a tumult of shouts, yells, blows and groans. We could only assume that they were being beaten to death. When the noise had died down, the door was flung open and a junior official from the Luan yamen entered and sat down, smoking his pipe. Others followed and with them he conversed in low tones, completely ignoring us the while. At length he rose and announced to us that as we "foreign devils" had caused such great suffering to the people of the neighbourhood, we were to be fined the sum of 200 ounces of silver and the sooner we paid up the better. To remonstrate was useless, though remonstrate we did. We respectfully reminded him that, as we had resided several years in the city, he must be aware that our teaching and manner of life were against evil-doing and that for him to take our money upon a false pretext was grossly unjust. Whereupon he sneeringly turned on his heel and went out with his following.

The afternoon of that long and bitter day was closing in and the twilight fast fading into darkness. What thoughts were ours in the gloom of our prison room! Betrayed, in the hands of the Boxers, our animals already killed and, for aught we knew to the contrary, our two companions also, and ourselves facing death—the situation could hardly have been darker. Just at the moment when the outlook was darkest, the door opened and in walked—Sheng-min! His appearance, just when we were mourning him as dead, was truly "light in the darkness", the earnest of our Father's future care for us, the promise of His mercy for dark days yet to come. It was not he and Pao-erh, after all, that had been beaten, but three men who had spoken up for us when we were condemned to die, declaring that the Boxers should not touch us! For this sentiment they had suffered a severe beating but had not actually been killed.

A lamp was now brought in and set in a niche in the wall above the table, at the head of which the same official as before seated himself with magisterial dignity to conduct the mock formality of a trial. We were forbidden to leave our places on the *kang*. No word was directly addressed to us and the proceedings consisted of a general indictment, supported by specific charges, sworn to by false witnesses—some of them too vile to put on paper. Among the more innocent were the hackneyed stories of cutting out children's eyes and hearts for purposes of alchemy, of bewitching the ground, spoiling the good luck and what not; reeled off in addition to those were charges of a more recent type: poisoning the wells, disturbing the repose of the Earth Dragon by the introduction of railways, shutting up the heavens, frustrating the prayers of the needy and blaspheming the gods. The dim flicker from the strand of cotton twist in oil, fell with uncertain light upon the livid faces of our accusers, revealing in part the passion that worked in every feature—a picture revolting enough at any time, but horrible in the distortions of semi-darkness. As charge after charge was brought forward and proved to the satisfaction of all, the excitement grew in intensity, until it reached the vehemence of fury. We were unanimously declared unfit to live and sentence of death was passed.

Forthwith they fell to discussing the mode and time of execution. The suggestions selected for consideration were: to poison us with opium there and then; to behead us with the sword in the inn yard; to shoot us with a foreign gun they had in their possession; or to carry us outside to the street and let the mob fall upon us. The last proposal found the most general acceptance and was accordingly adopted. Its great recommendation, apparently, was that it would give an opportunity to all who had a grudge against us to gratify their feelings of revenge. It would, above all, shift the responsibility for the crime from the shoulders of any known individuals to those of the nameless mob. The time chosen as most suitable for carrying the sentence into effect was daylight the following morning. And with that the dark conclave broke up.

Little did they know that there was One among them whom they knew not and against whom they were imagining vain things. Of a truth, we realized what it was to be "accounted as sheep for the slaughter"; but we also tasted in that solemn hour the triumph of the word, "Neither death . . . nor any other creature shall be able to separate us from the love of God, which is in Christ Jesus our Lord."

CHAPTER SEVEN

TUMULT

THE few remaining hours that were left to us before the death sentence was to be executed were, so far as our outward circumstances went, nothing but unrest. Ma, the official, took up his quarters in our room and with another close companion spread his bedding on the communal *kang*. Far into the night, there were many coming and going and the event of the morrow was freely and jestingly discussed before us. None was more offensively ribald than Ma himself.

Our persons and effects were now subjected to close scrutiny and search. Ma mounted the *kang* and with his own hands felt each article in turn. At last he came upon what he wanted—silver! With the exultant greed of a miser he clutched the packet and said, "You 'foreign devils' will have to make this up to two hundred taels before we have done with you. Where's the rest?" As there was nothing to be gained by resistance, we quietly surrendered our remaining store of silver, though not without rebuking the sin. Ignoring our remonstrance, he sent for scales and, surrounded by some half-dozen sycophants, he carefully checked the weights of the ingots. The sordid features of the intent group and the dirt-begrimed, cobwebbed room gave the impression of a veritable den of thieves, which in fact it was. I understood

then, as never before, how the love of money can be said
to be "the root of all evil". Every unholy passion lurked
in the lust depicted on their faces.

When the weight was told, it was declared to be in-
sufficient. "Come, bring out the rest of your money, or it
will be the worse for you!" said Ma. We replied that he
already had all and that if he did not believe us he could
search us and see. Whereupon he and his companions
searched our persons. Finding nothing, he said, "Very
well, if you can't make it up in money, you will have to
make it up in kind." And they fell to appropriating whatever their heart coveted amongst our goods on the bed.
Still they were not satisfied. Seeing that they were about
to search our persons again, we gave up the last valuables
we had—our watches and my pocket-knife. These were
considered a great find, but soon they wanted more.
"What we have here will not bring the amount up to a
hundred and fifty ounces. So your things in the litters are
forfeit also." No need to be told that! We had guessed it
long before. It was merely another attempt at "saving
their face" over a shameless piece of wholesale robbery,
determined upon from the beginning.

Having thus justified themselves in their wickedness,
they lay down beside us, not to sleep, but to regale themselves with opium and to gloat over the spoil, Ma fondling
the large fifty ounce "shoe" of silver and examining the
names on it in the light of his opium lamp.

I suppose it must have been about three o'clock in the
morning when a man with a large yamen lantern came
in, evidently to receive instructions. Almost immediately
after he had withdrawn, the deep boom of a gong broke

out upon the stillness and continued at intervals until it was light.

For all this the grace of God sufficed us. Notwithstanding the intense heat, the lively vermin and the opium fumes, my dear wife was given a spell of quiet sleep for which I could not sufficiently thank the gracious Giver. For the rest, we spoke but little and that only in whispers, that we might not arouse the suspicions of our captors. In the near prospect of a violent death, however, we each experienced the deep peace of the words, "I know whom I have believed, and am persuaded that He is able to keep that which I have committed unto Him."

While it was yet dark, the summons of the gong caused a stirring which made itself heard outside. Every now and then the door would open and two or three would look in, leer at us, exchange a few words with Ma and go out. These, doubtless, had to do with the business in hand. Then, as the grey of early dawn appeared, the inn yard began to fill; and with the broadening daylight the whole place was alive with thronging crowds. Ma went out to supervise the final preparations. Silently my wife and I took the last secret farewell of each other. The glory of which she whispered to me was even now in her face and the tender firmness of her hand's pressure told me how completely she was lifted above the fear of death. Only when she kissed her little son and daughter goodbye did her eyes moisten—that was all. We commended one another into the hands of our Father in prayer in expectation of imminent death; but, even as I prayed, the petition seemed forced from my lips, "If it is not Thy will that we should die at this time, then, O our God, for the glory of Thy great name bring their counsel to nought and weaken their arm!''

Almost immediately, Ma entered with his following and in peremptory tones ordered us out to the litters. I led the way with Hedley, followed by my wife and Hope. At this point Ma's impatience could no longer brook restraint and brutally seizing Miss Gates by the hair, he dragged her from the bed and thrust her to the door with a blow from his clenched fist.

We were scarcely allowed time to seat ourselves before the signal to move was given. Our attendants were dragged back and not allowed to go with us. So far as I could see from the front litter, all three litters started off together, my wife's being close behind. As we passed out of the courtyard into the street, what a sight met our gaze! The roadway for the first hundred yards was held by Boxer guards, armed with sword and spear, and brave in Boxer red: while on either side, as far as the eye could see, was massed in dense formation a great multitude, eagerly expectant, and armed—apparently to a man—with some rude implement or other.

No sooner had we cleared the inn gate than the mob closed in upon us. Then we were halted and they formed themselves into a procession headed by Ma. A young man with a large gong stationed himself beside my litter. When all was ready marshalled, at a signal from the official the procession moved forward to the measured beat of the gong. Stealing a glance behind I saw that the other litters were following, lurching from side to side amidst the crowd.

We had traversed about two-thirds of the long main

street when an extraordinary commotion ensued. The official Ma dashed at my leading mule's head and tearing at his mouth forced a halt. Then, in orthodox Chinese style, he raged and cursed and denounced the people for their "peaceableness" and for having "ruined the whole business". What he was talking about I could not understand at the time. But evidently the preconcerted signal for attack had met with no response.

Ma's rage yielded at last to the persuasive vehemence of those about him as they urged him to have us taken to the boundary of the town where they would themselves finish the matter to his satisfaction. Whereupon the procession moved forward and we were rapidly borne on outside the gate. We were well outside when Ma thrust his head into my litter and said, "Throw out your bedding roll, quick!" This was easier said than done. Not merely was it a heavy, awkward article in itself, but it formed our seat and how to dislodge it was a problem. However, Ma appreciated the difficulty as much as I did and without further ado set to work to solve it with his own hands. Once the unwieldy bulk had lumped over the side, I found myself sitting on the hard boxes in the ropework below. In trying to readjust our position, I frightened the animals who began to kick and plunge in such a way that I took Hedley and jumped to the ground. Not a moment too soon for the litter was almost immediately crumpled up and demolished. I looked around for the other litters. Miss Gates' litter was nowhere to be seen and I concluded that she must be dead, but there about twenty yards away was my wife's and between us a howling mob besetting her on every side. Suddenly, between the stampeding mules, the litter heaved over and fell to the ground. I saw, too, the knives with which the bystanders slashed at the cordage to get at the boxes and I cried to God for the protection of my wife and little Hope. Then from the midst of the fanatical mass they both emerged. I sprang forward to meet her. Her hair was dishevelled and her face ashy white, but she was perfectly calm and unscathed. There were bruises and torn clothing, but not a wound, not a scratch and Hope was as calm as her mother. Not only so, but to complete the marvel, Miss Gates was with them, unhurt and calm as they!

There was nothing, however, in our circumstances to suggest that we had escaped or could eventually escape the death to which we had been sentenced. When once the litters were wrecked, it did not take long to dispose of their contents; as soon as one and another possessed themselves of what they wanted or could lay hands on, they made off with their ill-gotten gains. To our amazement, they were soon hurrying in all directions as if in flight and we were left standing alone! In a few minutes there was nothing left of the great throng that had carried us out to death save a few scattered groups in twos and threes watching us from a distance.

Among those who made off was the redoubtable Ma. Just at the moment when I was standing with Hedley by the wrecked litter, he had dashed upon me suddenly from amongst the crowd, his face livid with passion, and, dealing me a staggering blow, ordered me to show him whether I had yet any secret possessions upon my person. I quietly opened my tunic and he caught sight of the small pocket attached to my girdle in which I carried my consular passport. Thrusting in his hand, he drew forth the document. One glance at the heading sufficed to show him its purport and with a malicious gleam he tore it to pieces before my eyes. Then, ordering me to give up the pouch, empty as it was, he took it and was gone. And that was the last I saw of Mandarin Ma.

Thus miraculously ended one of the most critical episodes of that critical period. When one considers that the extermination of the "foreign devil" was the express object of the Boxer organization, and that we were actually in their hands, the fact that the Boxer soldiery never came near us is inexplicable on any other ground than that of Divine intervention. We read in it the answer to the prayer we had offered in the room in the early hours of the morning.

"Associate yourselves, O ye people, and ye shall be broken in pieces; . . . take counsel together and it shall come to nought; . . . for God is with us."

CHAPTER EIGHT

NAKEDNESS

THE situation in which we now found ourselves called indeed for a fresh committal of our way to God. Here we were, with our life yet whole in us, it is true, but robbed of every earthly possession, without so much as a "cash" with which to buy food. We were desperately hungry after our long fast. We were, moreover, still in the midst of those whose resentment towards us burned as fiercely as ever. Whither should we turn? In deep perplexity, we looked up and very simply asked God to lead us. We were consciously shut up to Him even for the literal putting of one foot before the other.

After prayer, it became clear to us that we should return to Hantien where we would probably be safer than on the open road. And if our Chinese companions were alive, they would find us more easily there than elsewhere. We hoped also that someone might take pity on us and give the children at least a morsel of food.

Thus we turned and went back. Wearily we entered the gate and sat down on a stone block about twenty yards inside. The long street was almost deserted—strange contrast to the scene of an hour or so before! It all seemed like a dream, but for the fact of our all too palpable destitution. Here and there were small groups of men and immediately opposite a group of women were curiously eyeing us. Finally Miss Gates spoke to them, entreating their compassion and begging for just a drink of water. At the sound of her voice, they looked scared and retreated into the safe seclusion of the doorway. There was nothing to do but to sit on, with no protection from the scorching sun. Anxiously we hoped to see our Chinese companions again, for it seemed to us now that their presence was indispensable to our safety and survival. Our hearts sickened with hope deferred.

Meanwhile the situation was becoming awkward again. The riff-raff who had been hanging about the outskirts of the town in expectation that we would turn our steps away from it and towards the country, began to collect and gather round us. We concluded that it was time to be making a move. Yet what move could we make? As we were preparing to start, who should push his way through the ring but Sheng-min! The comfort and joy of seeing the dear lad again were immense. He took in the situation at a glance and said, "Come quickly, we must be going."

The bystanders fell back sullenly as we rose and no one even followed us as we passed out through the gate into the open once more. We walked on until we came to a place where there was a choice of roads: the main road bore to the left and a kind of bridle path led through a gully. We decided to take the latter as affording greater possibilities for eluding observation. But we could not escape so easily. First two tramps recognized us and then, as we rejoined the main road, an armed band of Hantien men caught sight of us. So we returned to the gully where the forlornness of our condition almost overwhelmed me. We were seven hundred miles from the nearest place of refuge, we had been stripped of all our money and possessions and were without any means of conveyance.

When we emerged from the gully, a small village was before us, about half a mile distant, called Shahokou. A crowd of men and lads was awaiting us, all carrying some kind of weapon—hoes, sickles, knives and the like. Once more we resigned ourselves to die and quietly sat down by the roadside to await the end. From behind us the Hantien crowd came to join our new tormentors. One of the tramps was still dogging our steps too and he now ordered us on, directing us to a small booth by the wayside where we were glad of the shelter provided from the midday sun. But the owner would not let us stay and we had to move to a grassy slope further on where a group of saplings afforded some shade. The crowd followed us and for the next hour or two threatened us over and over again with death, mingling coarse mockery with their threats. The moving spirit was the wicked tramp. "We'll strip them first and then break their heads," we heard him say, and the word was taken up and passed around. At one point a passing Boxer officer joined the crowd and urged them on to do the deed at once; when they failed to do so, he went off promising to bring back with him some other Boxers to deal with us.

Meanwhile, Sheng-min had been able to procure two three-cornered cakes of rice and dates for the children who, like ourselves, had been without food for twenty-six hours. Their eyes glistened at the sight of the tempting morsels. As the cakes reached their mouths, one who had been increasingly obnoxious snatched them away and ate them before the children. By this act, the barrier of restraint was broken down and the one cowardly deed

F

was followed by another. The man standing immediately in front of my wife suddenly darted forward and seizing her left hand attempted to tear the wedding ring from her finger. I just whispered, "Let it go, darling. Don't grieve over it. The Lord will give you much more than this." So, meekly opening her hand, she yielded up the treasure.

This overt act of violence was the signal for a general attack. With a wild shout of "Rob!" they rushed upon us. There was not a moment to think how one should act. We were each seized and hurled out into the road, into the midst of the raging mass. By a painful process not far removed from lynching, my clothes were torn from me and when they had finished with me I was naked save for socks and an undervest. But I had little thought for my own condition. Where was my wife? I caught sight of her standing alone, anxiously looking for her children. She was flushed from the violence with which she had been handled; her gown was gone and her Chinese under blouse and nether garments were torn. But she was not seriously injured and greeted me with, "Oh, thank God you are alive!" and then, "Have you seen the children? Oh, where are they?"

It was a heart-rending sight when, a moment or two later, we did see them. Not dead, thank God, nor, apparently, injured, but in uttermost terror and bewilderment, wringing their hands and crying piteously for us, as they ran distractedly hither and thither among the mob. Their joy at seeing us seemed to eclipse all their terror and very soon the tears were forgotten in the comfort of having their hands fast in ours again. Nothing had been left to them save their light combinations and socks.

And Miss Gates? She was lying in the roadway some thirty yards off, stripped of her gown, face downwards and quite motionless. We thought at first she was dead, but Sheng-min was with her and, as I went forward, he raised her and she opened her eyes. Presently, with his support, she was able to move and together we retraced our steps to the booth where we were allowed a seat on a low plank beside the door of the food-shop. There we briefly exchanged accounts of our experiences: the two women had been knocked down and hauled along the ground, Miss Gates becoming unconscious from a violent blow on the head. The children had been cruelly mauled and even threatened with a sword, "But," said Hope, "I asked God not to let him hurt me and he went away!"

We had reached about the lowest point of distress and humiliation. It was my wife who reminded me that this was the fellowship of Christ's sufferings and that He was counting us worthy to suffer shame for His name.

Some degree of pity at the sight of our misery had been excited in the hearts of a few and a bowl of thin millet gruel was passed out to us. For this we heartily thanked God, praying that He would bless the giver. Later, a short coat of filthy rags, such as professional beggars wear, was handed to me over the heads of the bystanders from within the shop. The donor was none other than the tramp, himself now arrayed respectably in my gown! So now our friend had achieved his object: he had my garment and I could have his. He and I had changed places. It would have required much grace, under ordinary circumstances, even to have handled such a disgusting, lice-infested thing; but as it was, I had to be grateful for any covering at all for my nakedness. Bowing my acknowledgments to the man, I quickly put it on.

Yet a little later, one of my stolen shoes was returned, and this proved of the greatest service to me afterwards. The dear children's shoes were also recovered. The kindness of the Lord was crowned by the arrival of the other boy Pao-erh on the scene with a pair of pants of his own for me. They were well patched and far too small, but what of that? They met my sore need and, more than that, they were the expression of the love of Christ, offered me in His name and for His sake. As I thanked the dear lad, I thought with joy of the King's recognition awaiting him: "I was naked, and ye clothed Me. Inasmuch as ye have done it unto one of the least of these My brethren, ye have done it unto Me. Come, ye blessed of My Father."

CHAPTER NINE

TENDER MERCIES

THE day was wearing to a late afternoon. The first part of the programme which the people had set themselves had been completed: we had been stripped. The stripping doubtless was but the prelude to the killing. This was but a brief respite, not a reprieve. A clear indication of this seemed to be given when the shopkeeper came out and once more ordered us off the premises. There was nothing to do but to return to our former seat among the saplings.

As we sat I need hardly say we prayed, not so much for ourselves as for our would-be murderers. It was no light compensation for the bitterness of the cross that we should be given also, by His grace, the fellowship of His constraining love; and even the very prayer from His own Cross, "Father, forgive them; for they know not what they do." To find it possible to be possessed at such a time by the spirit of divine love and compassion instead of the natural spirit of resentment and hate, was to us a tangible evidence of the truth of the Gospel we had preached, such as no philosophy in the world could explain away.

Over and over again passages of Holy Scripture were brought vividly and appropriately to our minds. It was as if Jesus drew near and talked with us by the way; and the words that He spoke to us were spirit and life. It was literally as though I heard His living voice beside me.

And now, at this new juncture, He was breathing in my ear, "Be not afraid of them that kill the body, and after that have no more that they can do; but . . . fear Him, which after He hath killed hath power to cast into hell; yea, I say unto you, fear Him." And I knew it for my Lord's own voice when the words echoed within, "Said I not unto thee that, if thou wouldest believe, thou shouldest see the glory of God?"

How graciously and abundantly He met my expectation! I proved the literal truth of His words; for I bear record that He gave me such a sight of the glory of God as to eclipse the sight of death and to deliver me from all my fears.

How long we continued to sit there I cannot say. The time seemed interminable. The sun was dropping to the west and still the mob held back and the Boxers had not returned. At length, to my amazement, one of the men, probably a village elder, called to us:

"What are you sitting there for? We don't want you here. Be off with you! Go away!"

The cry, "Go away, go away!" was taken up and I saw our God-given opportunity.

"We have no wish to stay here," I said. "If my respected elder brother will allow us to go quietly on our way, we will go at once."

We got up and moved off. Once more the crowd fell back before us as if held by some unseen Power and not a hand was lifted to touch us as we passed on to the Kaoping road.

We had not gone far, however, before they caught up with us again and made it pretty clear that they intended to dog our steps. Upon this, we again seated ourselves on a grassy sward by the roadside; to attempt to go on with these people at our backs seemed foolish. Once more they crowded around us.

Among the most treasured possessions which we had lost with our other things was my wife's pocket Bible. As we sat, we suddenly caught sight of it in the hands of our old friend the tramp who was idly toying with it or showing it to his neighbours. He refused all our pleas for its return and the last I saw of it was its disappearance—most sad irony—into the pocket of my gown which he was wearing! But what saddened our hearts most of all was the contemptuous reception given to our presentation of the Gospel story in response to their questions.

"Jesus, Jesus," one old man thundered; "what do we want with your Jesus? We mean to drive you 'foreign devils' out of China and Jesus too. Away with Him, and away with you! Go away!"

It now seemed that the end could not long be delayed. The crowd made a threatening move towards us as they again took up the cry "Go! go!" We answered as before in polite, conciliatory tones, that we had no wish to trouble them with our presence but that it was they who would not allow us to go.

Once again they fell back and we rose to go. They made no attempt to follow us, and when we looked behind at the bend of the road, there was no one to be seen. To escape attention we left the road they had seen us take and made for the fields. There was a sharp shower of rain and we were soon wet to the skin. But even in this we saw the good hand of God, because the rain would both deter the people from coming after us for a while and also show them how false was the superstitious charge they had brought against us. When the rain stopped, I turned and, to my dismay, saw on the skyline the figures of scouts on the look-out and I knew that we had been seen. Immediately we moved out of sight on to some lower ground and decided to hide ourselves for a while in a small hollow off the beaten track, screened by shrubs. It was nearly sunset and we hoped that we might get away later under cover of darkness. Soon we heard voices as searchers passed us by and, unfortunately for us, two men happened to see us in the shallow depression and ran off to report. Weary, rain-bedraggled and so hungry, we were sorely dejected as we went slowly on, when the Lord gave us a token for good. Two men were coming towards us: whether friend or foe we knew not. Sheng-min answered their call and then told us to have no fear. One of the men was a gentleman from Luan and with real compassion in his voice, he said,

"I am so sorry for you. I would like to help you, but am helpless to do so. Certain death awaits you: you cannot escape. There are people all around. But I would urge you, under any circumstances, to avoid the village ahead of you. Yet I know that you cannot go far without losing your lives. It is very, very hard for you!"

And with that he handed me twenty-five cash, saying, "Take this: it is all I have on me."

His companion then came forward and with a "I am sorry for you!" thrust into my hand a tin of condensed milk which he had recovered from the plundered supply of our litters. Thanking them warmly in the name of the

Lord Jesus, we turned our steps in another direction, towards the village of Wangfang where one of the church evangelists lived. There we hoped it might be possible to hide until the storm had blown over.

But our change of direction was quickly noted and the chase began afresh. They now actually attacked Sheng-min, overpowered him and as he lay on the ground we thought that he would be killed. Others went for Pao-erh, but as he put up no resistance, they were content with searching him and robbing him of the little silver he had. This was the silver which, unknown to us, he and Sheng-min had managed to secrete on their persons at Hantien and had jealously guarded until now. Sheng-min's life had been spared when his assailant's attention was distracted by the silver, though he had received a rough handling in the scuffle.

As we went on, we met a small group of people, and a woman of their number, touched at the sight of the pitiable condition of my wife and Miss Gates, offered to repair the rents in the garments left to them.

These little acts of kindness moved us deeply and the continued presence with us of the two boys hitherto had been an untold comfort. But we were about to lose one of them. Without saying a word, Pao-erh pressed on ahead, and we thought that he was going on to reconnoitre. But we never saw him again. This was a sore trial, yet the Lord was our confidence and we rested in the assurance that He was ordering all things in perfect wisdom.

CHAPTER TEN

FLIGHT BY MOONLIGHT

W E were soon approaching another village along a steep road which fell away on one side down to a dry torrent bed. The usual crowds were gaping at us and among them a sprinkling of the more respectable elements as well as the riff-raff. It was almost dark and we found ourselves being jostled towards the village temple. For the second time that day we heard the ominous boom of the processional gong. Sheng-min stopped immediately and whispered:

"Don't go on! They mean to stone you to death here. Turn back quickly!"

That was impossible with the dense crowd urging us on from behind and with great presence of mind Sheng-min whispered:

"Down the slope—quick! Follow the track!"

Instantly we stepped off the road and in the dusk dropped down the hill in single file winding among the rocks and shrubs. The mob had stopped dead at the top of the slope and there was now a deathly silence, as spellbound they watched us slipping away from under their very hand. We were soon out of sight and hurrying on with strength divinely renewed. Sheng-min brought up the rear and before us in the bright moonlight there was nothing but the white zigzag of the trail and the gleaming breadth of the torrent bed. On we sped with wondering hearts, in the consciousness that God had, for the third time at least that day, wrought for us a great deliverance. Wangfang was the near goal before us and every step was bringing it nearer.

But we were not alone! I suddenly caught sight of four stealthy figures keeping parallel with us on the other side of the river bed. Ere long they came out into the open moonlight and casually accosted us, asking, as is usual on the road in China, where we had come from and whither we were bound. We noticed that they were armed with pole-axes and a certain smartness of bearing suggested that these were soldiers and probably Boxers. Sheng-min recollected a man in the crowd calling him aside to tell him that the Boxers were plotting to kill us at the bed of the river.

We were very weary by now and called for a halt. The men too sat down, some distance away. This was our first opportunity to open the milk tin and give the children a tiny quantity of the precious food, the only sustenance they had had since noon of the preceding day. By common consent we were to keep it entirely for the children's use, for we were again penniless after losing the twenty-five cash with the silver in Sheng-min's care.

After a brief rest we stood up to go on. The men arose too and went on to wait for us at a point where the torrent bed was intersected by cross-roads. What awaited us now? As we came up to them, they confronted us with an insolent demand for money. They could not believe our assurance that we had not a penny. We all sat down while Sheng-min argued and explained, the altercation going on for about an hour. While Sheng-min talked, we spent the time in silent prayer. Every now and then, one of the men, who were certainly Boxers, would spring to his feet with a curse and stand over us with his pole-axe, threatening to strike, but finding that threats were of no avail, he would sit down again.

Miss Gates, who had the advantage of being able to understand every word that was being spoken, said:

"Unless God works a miracle for us, we shall not leave this spot alive."

So we made our prayer in the name of the Lord that He would take every one of these men right away. As we prayed we saw the figures of some more men coming from the opposite side of the river and soon there were about a dozen or fifteen gathered at the knoll where we were sitting. Apparently they were just foot passengers on their way home, attracted by the unusual gathering in the moonlight. Their sympathies were soon enlisted on the side of the Boxers, who were emboldened by their arrival. We were told that if their demands were not met we should be stripped of the last shred of clothing. When this and other menacing gestures failed, two of the new-comers approached my wife and Miss Gates and said that they were to be stripped first if we did not give them information about our money. There was a moment of hesitation and then the two women were seized by the throat and their upper garments torn from them. Miss Gates retained a thin vest but my wife was left naked to the waist.

As the men faced us again with the garments in their hands, I looked at them and said:

"You are human beings, it is true; but you have not the

feelings of your kind!"—about as stinging a reproach as one could address to a Chinese and containing a legitimate rebuke. I am bound to say that I was not prepared for the effect it produced. My remark went home like an arrow to the mark. They sullenly flung back the garments to their owners and one by one melted away, leaving only the four Boxers. After exchanging a few sentences with them and refusing a demand to follow them back to Luan, we watched them also shoulder their weapons and depart. Our prayer was thus fully answered and to God we ascribed the honour due to His name.

The moment the last of the men was out of sight, Sheng-min said:

"They are gone! Praise the Lord! Now come quick: we have not a moment to lose!" It must have been about eleven o'clock.

While he took Hedley in his arms, I took Hope and, in the light of the full moon, we hastened along in full flight. As the white blouses of the ladies made us conspicuous, Sheng-min thoughtfully threw his own dark blue coat over Miss Gates' shoulders and his black inner jacket over my wife's.

Tracing the river course up to the Wangfang hills, we found increasing cover provided by wooded undulations and coppices of thick undergrowth and we began to look for a resting and dark hiding place for the night. This we found in a graveyard with its dark cypress trees and monumental stones. There in the deepest shadows we could find we laid our weary bodies down at midnight and, in the peace of God, under the shadow of His wings, we slept.

Alas, we had been sleeping for probably less than an hour when Miss Gates was awakened by the shouts of the Boxers in their search for us. She roused us and it was clear that the men had returned with reinforcements. As we lay perfectly quiet and still, they passed very close to us. But though we were undiscovered we knew that we were in danger again. It was now out of the question to go on to Wangfang and so Sheng-min said he would try to find a cave in the locality known to him.

Refreshed by even the brief snatch of sleep, we moved out from the graveyard and its sheltering cypresses into the brilliant moonlight. But as we did so, some heavy clouds rolled up and hid the moon, which did not come out again until we were in a place of comparative safety.

How can I describe that weird and awful midnight tramp? We kept to the fields and sought the concealment of grove and coppice. Now we were climbing walls of ragged stone; now plodding over ploughed fields or struggling with stunted undergrowth. Sometimes it was so dark that we could scarcely see one another. And then, to our dismay, Sheng-min found that he had lost his bearings and the hope of reaching the cave was gone. All he could think of now was the shelter of some rural temple. Catching sight of one ahead, he went forward to investigate, only to find it full of the very men who were hunting our lives. Back we went towards the only resources still open to us—the hills.

Happily, the children were sound asleep and past all thought of crying and complaint, though their dead weight in our arms made progress slow and exhausting. After some while, the cover was broken by a gully cutting the coppice. Quickly crossing the gully, we traversed the coppice on the other side and found ourselves on the right hill slope. Slowly and painfully we made the ascent and with feelings of utter relief reached the summit at last. Here there was a round depression, deep enough to allow us to sit down and even stand without being seen. Into this basin we crept. A few minutes sufficed to make the needed preparations for a short night's rest and with stones for our pillows we lay down to sleep, in the assurance that He who had been so marvellously about our path was also about our bed.

CHAPTER ELEVEN

IN THE MOUNT WITH GOD

THE Luan plateau lies at about three thousand feet above sea level. However hot the days, the nights are cool, even in mid-summer. Consequently, in our semi-naked condition, without coverlets of any kind and exposed as we were at the top of a hill, we all suffered from intense cold. We huddled together as close as we could to keep in the vital heat, with the children wedged in between, doing our best to make our own single garments serve also as some kind of covering for them. But in vain. For myself, I know my teeth never stopped chattering all the night through. Sleep there was none for any of us, save the children.

Far away down in the distance, we heard the hoarse shouts of our pursuers as they pressed the chase, almost till break of day. Then followed a sweet spell of restful stillness, relieved of all unquiet alarms and with a consciousness of God's sheltering wings.

But this brief respite was followed by one of the worst crises in our experience. Among the many spots which I can look back upon as "holy ground", I think that that mountain top stands out pre-eminently. In very truth it was the mount of the Lord in which "He was seen"—the "holy mount" where we "were with Him"; and by a striking coincidence of His pleasure, the day was His own day, Sunday, July 8th.

The sunrise was one of glorious splendour. As the huge

disc of fiery red showed above the horizon, its colour seemed prophetic of what the day would bring for us of fiery trial. Not a cloud flecked the sky as, higher and higher, it rose into the azure.

After the bitter cold of the night, the genial warmth of its early rays was very comforting. But ere long, as its strength increased, it became a source of grave anxiety and distress, our summit being entirely destitute of tree life or shade of any kind. The children wakened early, but we dared not stir from the two positions of lying or sitting, nor durst we speak in tones above a whisper. From a child's point of view, such a prospect was far from cheerful. Yet they were wonderfully obedient when we explained to them the reason why.

After uniting in prayer, we began to think of breakfast —or rather the lack of it. It was just forty-two hours since anything solid had passed our lips. That was on Friday at noon. And here we were, fugitives in hiding, without sustenance or hope of getting any. It was wonderful how we were kept from suffering excessive pangs of hunger. We made the best of our circumstances and reminded ourselves that "Your Father knoweth what things ye have need of before ye ask Him". We were sure that, even if we had to eat the grass around us, He would so order it that the grass would sustain us. Thus the dear children, happy in having something to do, began to see what delicacies they could find among the weeds for breakfast. To their delight they were able to find several kinds which they gave out as "meat", with the leaves of the wild date shrub for "bread". Then lifting our hearts in thanksgiving to our Father, in the name of the Lord Jesus, and asking

G

His blessing upon what He had graciously given in our extremity, we made our herbal meal.

By about seven o'clock, according to the sun, its power was becoming perceptible and as it increased in intensity, we began to feel the absence of shelter. It was not long before the exposed parts of the children's bodies, their arms and legs, were burning red as from a scald. As the moisture of the skin dried, so also did that of the tongue and soon a great thirst was upon us. The trial of hunger was as nothing compared with this, for which there was no assuagement at all. The little ones' plaint, "I am so thirsty; please give me something to drink", soon became a piteous cry, "O Father! do give me water! Mother, won't you give me water?" We sought to hush them tenderly, for they could no longer refrain from crying aloud in their distress and we knew that this might easily lead to our discovery.

"Don't cry, darlings. We will ask God to send us water and we will be patient till He does."

The simple laying of our need before our Father comforted them, and it was touching to see how heroically they wiped their eyes and set themselves to "try to be good". We strove to divert their thoughts from their distress in various ways, but presently the piteous cry broke out again. And so it went on, with increasing distress to us all, especially my wife. As the time went by, our precious little Hope was unable to control herself. Her involuntary wail, "Father, Mother, water, water!"—continuing without intermittence as long as she was able to articulate—tore our very heart-strings. As for Hedley, when he saw the effect of his complaints upon us, he set himself determinedly to absolute silence. There he sat at his mother's side without so much as a murmur or a moan passing his lips. For hours, through all that burning heat, with his mouth parched and his limbs scorched, he sat quietly on, resolutely toying with the grass, a very miracle of self-control.

At length we could bear the sight of our little ones' sufferings no longer and we sent Sheng-min to the edge of the ring to survey the country. The news that he could see a rivulet about a mile from the foot of the hill only seemed to mock our grief. How was it possible to get the longed-for draught? Reluctant as we were to allow Sheng-min away from us, it now seemed the only thing to do to send him to try to bring back water. From the human standpoint, all our hopes, even of life itself, centred in him. Is it any wonder, therefore, that when the boy had disappeared from sight, a great sense of loneliness came over us, a horror of great darkness. The hour had come which was to be peculiarly the hour of our temptation.

Under the pressure of hunger, thirst and burning heat, my dear wife began to show signs of exhaustion, which made me apprehensive, to say the least. Pitilessly the sun poured down its rays of fire. It was imperative to improvise some slight shelter for her and the children. So Miss Gates and I divested ourselves of our upper garments and together held them over the heads of the other three. With the alleviation thus afforded, slender though it was, my dear one was not a little comforted and strengthened to hold on.

As the sun mounted towards the zenith, darkness

gathered over my soul. I think we were each one conscious of the same experience. It was not difficult to believe that Satan had been desiring to have us that he might sift us as wheat. That hallowed sense of our Lord's near Presence, which had hitherto solaced us and given us power to endure, was now withdrawn; and the language of our hearts was "Oh that I knew where I might find Him!" Yet all the while the Lord was near, though for the time being He willed, for His own great name's sake, that our eyes should be holden that we should not know Him.

Higher and higher rose the sun into the heavens and Sheng-min had not returned. Narrower and narrower grew the shadow thrown by our slender screen. Soon there would be no shadow at all. The children were barely covered by it now; but they seemed past noticing anything. A distressing phase of the situation was that with the increasing thirst, the saliva in the mouth turned to a viscous consistency, very difficult to get rid of. If water did not arrive soon, articulation would become impossible; even now it was often difficult to disengage the tongue from the palate.

In that hour all God's waves and billows seemed to go over me. As the sun poured its fiery heat upon us from above, the Wicked One hurled his fiery darts at us from beneath. How often I fell back upon the word, "I have prayed for thee that thy faith fail not." Over and over again I said to the Accuser, "Though He slay me, yet will I trust Him."

The Enemy's answer to all this was the collapse of my beloved Flora. She too had known the bitterness of those hours of darkness; but the language of her unwavering faith had been, "My flesh and my heart faileth; but God is the strength of my heart and my portion for ever." The sight of her steadfast endurance and the sweet, unmurmuring resignation to the will of God had been an unspeakable inspiration to me on that mountain top, during those hours of fierce temptation. And now she lay prostrate before me, overborne by physical weakness and deeply troubled in soul. As I watched her panting and gasping for breath, with no power to alleviate her suffering beyond supporting her head, it seemed as though I heard the serpent's hiss, "Yea, hath God said . . . ? Where are His promised mercies now? Has He not forgotten to be gracious?" In an agony of soul, my dear wife cried out from the deep darkness, "Oh, God has forsaken us! It can only be that we are not in His will or He would surely never have allowed us to come to this." Her distress, physically, was such that I felt sure she was dying; but it was as nothing to the trouble of her soul.

Scarcely had the words of anguish passed my precious one's lips than God put into Miss Gates' mouth the most wonderful song of praise I have ever heard. Kneeling by the side of her prostrate sister and holding her hand, she poured forth passage after passage, promise after promise, from the Scriptures, exalting His name, declaring His faithfulness and proving His unchanging and unchangeable love, sworn to us in the everlasting covenant and sealed to us in the blood of His own beloved Son. Never shall I forget the music of that heavenly utterance. Instantly the darkness was past and the light was shining again. The expression in my wife's face of joy unspeakable and full of glory, where but a moment before it had been one of unspeakable anguish and distress, was an evident token of what God had wrought. With the tears coursing down her cheeks, she said, "Oh, I will never, never doubt Him again." From that moment her glorious faith never wavered for an instant, but through every future trial only went from strength to strength.

Then together we repeated right through—with parched lips and stammering tongues, but with hearts that had tasted the wine of heaven—the beautiful hymn, so true to our experience:

> How sweet the name of Jesus sounds
>   In a believer's ear!
> It soothes his sorrows, heals his wounds,
>   And drives away his fear.

The effect of this divine cordial upon my dear wife physically was nothing short of miraculous. From an apparently dying condition she suddenly revived and sat up with a restored vigour which amazed me. By this visitation of God's grace, our hearts were encouraged to wait for His deliverance from a situation which was just as critical as ever. It was past noon and there was still no sign of Sheng-min. The sun's blaze was fiercer than ever and the sensation of thirst was becoming intolerable. We now had the greatest difficulty in making ourselves understood. The situation reached a climax when Miss Gates, who had been the chosen instrument in God's hand of my dear wife's restoration, suddenly fell to the ground in a faint. It seemed as if this were a last revengeful thrust from our retreating foe.

All the old sense of helplessness came over me. But, as my wife and I were pleading with God for our sister's recovery, I heard a voice as distinctly as if it were spoken in my ear—"Up, get thee down and tarry not!" The impression was so deep and I was so certain that God had spoken that I said to my wife:

"Come, darling, we must gather up what strength remains to us and go down to the water. It is not the will of God that we should remain here any longer."

Then, taking Miss Gates by the arm, I bent over her and said, "Dear sister, we must be going without delay. In the name of the Lord Jesus, get up." In a moment, consciousness was restored and she rose up with strength renewed from on high.

With such a confirmation that the thing was of God and in the assurance that the Lord our God was going before us, we left our hiding place and once more ventured out into the open. There below us was the thin streak of silver glinting in the sunlight. What a joy it was to point it out to the children and to see the faintest smile dawn over the sad, suffering little features!

Slowly and painfully we took our way down, making use of such cover as we could find on the lower slopes; down to the ploughed fields below and across them in as direct a line as the ground would permit; down to the lowest level and then, by the shortest cut we could make, to the water's edge. Regardless now of whether we were seen or not, we fairly ran, not *to* the water, but *into* it. Oh the bliss of giving our precious little darlings the first draught, as we filled our hands and put them to their swollen lips! But the process was all too slow to satisfy the urgent need.

Wading into mid-stream, and putting our mouths to the surface, we drank and drank till the craving was satisfied. We scarcely noticed that the thin silver streak of the distant view was in reality nearer the colour of copper than silver; for the water was heavily charged with yellow silt. After drinking, our tongue and palate were coated with a thick layer of mud! However, that was a minor consideration now and those draughts could not have been more delicious if they had been the purest spring water. We sat in the cool shallows for a few minutes longer, bathing our hands and faces and then, with hearts full of gratitude, we sought a place where we could lie down unobserved.

Once more a heathen burial ground was to be the spot that should enshrine the memory of God's great goodness. What the delicious shade of those dark yew trees and the luxurious comfort of the high grass-grown mounds were to us after being exposed for seven hours at least to the undimmed blaze and sweltering heat of a mid-summer sun, no one can imagine. Not least of the wonders of that memorable day was our miraculous preservation from sunstroke. That we suffered terribly under the sun's power only proves the marvel. The skin peeled from our faces and the children's arms, from the shoulder to the elbow, were one huge blister. But the sun had no power to hurt us beyond that. The Lord had been our shade upon our right hand. Certain it is that the power that brought us out alive, or that enabled us to endure what we did, was of God alone. And when we left the hill, it was with the consciousness that there we had "seen the Lord".

CHAPTER TWELVE

ARRESTED AND BETRAYED

WE had scarcely settled down to the enjoyment of our quiet retreat, when we heard the sound of music proceeding from a temple not far away. Worship was evidently going on; and I was troubled to think that soon the worshippers would be out and perhaps coming our way. Then the boom of a gong announced a procession and a few minutes later we caught sight of the motley crew of yamen tatterdemalions heralding the approach of an official.

It was idle to hope that we could escape detection now, though we lay close to the ground and absolutely still. Sure enough, one of the runners caught sight of us, stopped, looked hard and called the attention of the others. They too stopped and stared. Then I caught the dreaded words, "Foreign devils!" We had been recognized and were again among unfriendly people.

As the Mandarin's chair came into view, he craned his neck to see what was attracting the attention of his minions and then sent a runner to investigate. This man needed to ask no questions and returned at once to his lord to report that there were "foreign devils" hiding in the graveyard. As it happened, the Mandarin was the sub-Prefect of Luan. He issued a peremptory order and a few minutes later a yamen cart with a canopy arrived, in charge of two soldiers, and we were ordered to get in.

Meanwhile Miss Gates had again relapsed into a prostrate condition. All she could do was to say that she felt too ill to move. The Mandarin repeated the command, adding that he had orders to escort us to the next magistracy of Kaoping. At first we were sceptical and suspected a Boxer ruse. But when he showed us an official safe-conduct pass and pointed to a bundle of clothing in the cart which he said was for us from his senior official, we were inclined to believe him. He said he had been searching for us all night and had just given up the search when we were found.

The Mandarin repeated an impatient "Get on the cart at once!" We had to make a quick decision. Obviously we could not live on as we were, tramping the road as beggars at the mercy of hostile crowds. Perhaps this was the Lord's provision for our salvation. If so we would live to praise the Lord; and if it was for death—well, we would die anyway. We decided to trust the Lord and take the cart.

In a few moments all five of us were packed in, Miss Gates being lifted to her seat by one of the soldiers. Almost before we could take in the turn of events, we were splashing through the water of our stream towards Wangfang, en route for Kaoping. Looking back we marvel at the way God timed events from His command to me on the hill-top to the arrival of the official and his cart. Twenty minutes later in coming down from the hilltop and we would have been too late! Moreover, had Shengmin returned to us there with water, we would doubtless have delayed longer in coming down and so missed the transport now provided.

We never saw Sheng-min again. We eventually learned that, being penniless, he had been unsuccessful in procuring any vessel in which to carry water. Moreover, he was recognized and accused of being a Roman Catholic. When he denied this he was tried by ordeal and kept until the late afternoon. The test failed, but when he returned to the hill-top he found that we had gone. Even then he only gave up the search after he had probed the hills and caves around in vain. He then went back to Luan and informed the sub-Prefect of the condition in which he had left us. He was told that a cart had already been sent to take us on, with clothing, ten ounces of silver and six thousand cash. The first part of this statement was true enough, but as far as we knew, the clothes, silver and cash were a myth. Thus Sheng-min's faithful and self-sacrificing ministry to us came to an end. Both he and Pao-erh had been given to us for just as long as they were needed. Now in these new circumstances of our arrest, when they could no longer serve us, they were withdrawn by the same gracious Hand that had given them to us.

The relief of finding ourselves under official surveillance after being for nearly three days exposed to mob law, was greater than I can express, especially as the assurances given to us provided grounds for hope. The mercy of a temporary shelter from the heat under the canopy of the cart and the knowledge that we were speeding in the right direction contributed to the raising of our spirits. The contrast to what, but an hour before, had been the grim prospect before us was amazing.

In their exhausted and famished condition, seated on

the bare boards of the springless cart, my wife and Miss Gates found the bumpy journey over the rough and deeply rutted roads a severe ordeal. We reached Wang-fang about 1.30 p.m. At the little food shop where we stopped, we were given the option of remaining in the shop on the street front or of going to the more private quarters at the back. The natural choice under the cir-cumstances was to go to the inner room and the escort seemed to approve. Passing through the shop, we were shown into a narrow, dingy room, thick with dust and dirt, on the farther side of the usual courtyard. By the officer's orders our wants were well supplied. Hot water was brought us to drink; and shall I ever forget the fragrance of the savoury pork dumplings that were set steaming hot before us! The sight of food—and such food—was quite overwhelming: and we thanked God for inclining the officer's heart towards us in this unexpected way. We ate it with a ravenous relish begotten of a fifty-hour fast; for, except for the mouthful of grass plucked on the hill-top at sunrise that day, we had tasted nothing since Friday at noon.

As the news of our arrival spread, so the courtyard began to fill with a curious, gaping crowd. When no move was made to continue the journey after the usual limit of a midday halt and there was no sign of our escort, my fears and misgivings returned. We noticed, too, that many of the crowd around us were wearing the badge of the "Big Sword Society" or Boxers. Soon, our door was shut from the outside and a Boxer sentry set to guard it. All kinds of questions filled our minds. And as the after-noon wore on, the suspicion of foul play increased. I began to reproach myself that I had perhaps fallen into a trap.

Outside our room was a passage and the constant coming and going suggested preparations for something or other—we knew not what. We feared the worst. I have already mentioned that, in happier times, we had visited Wangfang on our journeys and the people there had certainly heard the Gospel message. One of our evangelists actually lived there and we hoped against hope that we might see him or his wife.

Those who came into the courtyard now seemed too intent on what was going on to stand staring at us as before. We were therefore left more or less free of their company. A good many women had come in to see us at one time or another, and towards late afternoon, the door opened and a little woman hobbled across to the *kang* on her bound feet and climbed up beside my wife and Miss Gates. They recognized her as one whom they had seen in the evangelist's home and to whom they had spoken the Word of Life. In scarcely audible tones, she told them that the Boxers had been searching all the previous night for us and had ransacked the evangelist's house in the belief that we were hidden there. "And," she added, "I have come to tell you that they are now going to kill you here. You are all to be burned to death in this room and the evangelist's wife is to die with you. They are already piling the wood to fire the building. When all is ready, your friend will be brought across!" With an added "I feel very sorry for you" she slipped off the bed and hobbled quickly away.

Once again we were face to face with the king of

terrors; and once again we cried out of the depths to Him that is King even of that king and mighty to save. The same God who had delivered us at Icheng, at Hantien, at Shahokou, in the torrent bed and on the hill-top was with us still—"the same yesterday, and today and for ever".

If any doubts remained about the truth of the woman's words, they were removed by the entrance of the inn-keeper and his servant, who began to clear the room of every vestige of furniture, even to the straw mats from under the ladies on the bed. Then, when they had completed their task, the door was shut, the sentry mounted guard and we were alone in the despoiled room. Through a paperless square in the window-frame, I could see that our mule was still in the stall and I clung to the hope fostered by the animal's presence that the escort responsible for us had not deserted us. With what intensity I peered through that tiny square, watching every movement for fear of being outwitted by the mule's sudden removal.

Suddenly, I heard the back gate into the yard, close to which the mule was tethered, open. A man slipped in and quickly loosed the halter.

"Now or never: come at once!" I said.

Snatching up the children, we quietly opened the door, dashed past the unwary sentry and out of the open gate where we found our escort hurriedly preparing to put the mule in the shafts of the cart and to get away without us. Our unexpected appearance on the scene took them completely aback. For a moment they seemed dumbfounded. They could not deny that they were about to go, for we had caught them in the very act; and as they were bound by orders to take us on to Kaoping, they could not refuse to take us with them without "losing face".

At a shout, a large crowd had quickly gathered, yet not a soul attempted to touch us. It was evident that they too were nonplussed by this sudden counter-stroke. It was generally supposed that we were safely shut up and a prey ready to their hand.

Miss Gates' thorough knowledge of the local dialect now proved invaluable. The escort and those about them talked freely among themselves, never dreaming that any one of us was able to follow the drift of their rapid conversation. Our professed friends were clearly in collusion with the Boxers and had agreed to abandon us to their tender mercies. The programme having been so abruptly interfered with in this inconvenient way, they were now discussing how it could be remedied. Miss Gates heard them plan to work the animal up into such a restive state when we were about to mount the cart that it would bolt without us. Thus they would both secure their end and "save their face".

Miss Gates promptly conveyed this information and, realizing that our only chance was to get on the cart before the mule was harnessed, we all leapt up one by one, to the dismay of the escort and the amazement of all. The officer's bewilderment turned to fury as he and the soldiers cursed us and ordered us to dismount. Quietly Miss Gates told them that we knew all their plans and that as there had been a safe-conduct pass issued for our safe delivery at Kaoping, we were not going to leave the cart until we arrived there.

Once more they debated among themselves what to do.

Some proposed that we be roasted to death in the cart where we were, but the escort would not agree to involving themselves and yamen property in this way. They explained to us that the reason why they wanted us to dismount was so that they could get at their money and coats stowed away inside. To hand out the articles required was a very simple matter, and the chagrin of the men found vent in dark scowls and mutterings. When they saw that we were not to be moved by fair means or foul, the officer mounted his horse, the soldiers tore at the mule's mouth and off we dashed, amid the curses, hoots and yells of the mob.

As we careered down the street, we were pursued by hundreds of local Boxers shouting, "Death to the 'foreign devils'! They think they have escaped us: wait till they get to Yincheng and then see what will become of them!"

CHAPTER THIRTEEN

THE RESTRAINING HAND

THE Boxer mob followed us to the bounds of Wang-fang and then left us to pursue the journey to Yincheng unmolested. The welcome silence that now prevailed was in contrast to the fury of the storm that speeded our departure. When I recall the murderous looks and gestures of our pursuers as they ran alongside the cart, I marvel again at the power of the Hand that held them back and then dispersed them.

It must have been about 6 p.m. when we rattled into Yincheng. This was a coal-mining town of some size and importance which had been frequently visited on our evangelistic journeys. Only three months ago Dr. Hewitt and I had preached on the streets and distributed a quantity of Christian literature. How different my circumstances and appearance now! Worn with suffering, unshaven, with matted queue and clothed in beggar's rags, I was a prisoner on my way to execution!

Apparently the escort were anxious to keep the fact of our arrival dark as we entered by a quiet street and came to a halt almost immediately in front of some large closed gates. There was no loud knocking, but soon the gates opened and we drove into the courtyard of a comfortable inn. We were the only customers and as the gates closed behind us we hoped that we were to enjoy the boon of a sorely-needed night's rest in quietness. There was nothing to indicate trouble in spite of the parting shouts

H

of the Wangfang Boxers. A nice room was allotted to us and hot water brought us to drink. As we lay down on the *kang* we lifted our hearts in thankfulness to God.

We had not been reclining ten minutes before we heard shouting and battering at the gate. There was nothing for it but for the innkeeper to open and some dozen people pushed in to have a look at the "foreign devils". Others followed until our hopes of a peaceful night vanished. They stood in the room and those who could not get in tore the paper from the windows and fought for a glimpse of us. Things became so bad that the escort ordered us to sit outside on a form placed by the doorway so that all could see us.

On coming out into the open I was concerned to see that the large majority of the men and lads who faced us were dressed like rain processionists. Humanly speaking, nothing could have been more inopportune than our arrival during a rain procession. Severe penalties attached to crossing the line of such processions, even for Chinese; for "foreign devils" the penalty would be certain death.

We sat on the form for some time, patiently and courteously answering the insolent questions put to us. It was plain, however, that they had not come merely to gratify idle curiosity. Their insolence soon passed from words to deeds and they began to indulge in malicious horseplay. Seeing the trend of things, the officer ordered us into another room and locked us in. This was worse than at Wangfang, but protest was useless. All we could do was to remind the fellow that he was responsible for our protection and to assure him that we implicitly trusted him to bring us safely to Kaoping.

Outside our new prison there was a terrifying scene as these rain processionists glared in through the paperless windows and heaped curses on us. Our offence now was that we had not only caused the drought from which the people were suffering but, by arriving during the procession, we were frustrating the efficacy of their prayers. Finally, they would be frustrated no longer and with a riotous rush they forced the door and broke into the room.

What would have happened next I dare not think, had it not been for the concerted action of the officer and the landlord. The latter, anxious for his property, refused to have us on the premises any longer. He and the officer forced their way into the room and ordered us down from the *kang* and out into the courtyard. I demurred, realizing the danger of such a step. But the next instant I was torn from the others, dragged from the *kang* and hurled through the door out into the midst of the seething mass. But as no one touched me, I turned to see what had become of the others. With admirable courage my wife and Miss Gates had jumped from the *kang* the moment after my seizure and, dragging the children after them, were fighting their way through behind me. We were soon able to join hands.

Keeping tight hold of one another, we were irresistibly borne along outside the gates, at times being lifted off our feet by the pressure. Nothing but the sustaining power of God could have kept my wife and the children from serious injury. As we were swept into the road we were met by a cross current—the main body of processionists—and the result was a veritable mill race upon which we were carried like straws down the narrow street.

The officer of the escort was still quite near at hand—anxious to get rid of us, but in such a way as not to implicate himself. He was obviously trying to give us the slip. At my wife's suggestion, the two ladies seized his two hands and hung on, thus openly claiming his protection, an obligation he could not repudiate. Yet all the time Miss Gates could hear him discussing a way to be rid of us with others in the crowd. We were to be asked to sit down at a certain stony spot and that would be the signal for us to be trampled to death under the feet of the mob. Miss Gates therefore warned us on no account to accept any invitation to be seated.

By this time my estimate of the size of the huge crowd that swarmed about us was between eight and ten thousand. The whole countryside was in town for the procession. We eventually arrived at the agreed "stony spot" and as if by common consent the great procession stopped too. The officer then said that, as we might have to wait some considerable time for the cart, we had better sit down awhile. We thanked him, but replied that we would prefer to keep with him and remain standing. His look of utter bewilderment was almost pathetic. The sweat broke out in great drops on his forehead. He was torn between his desire to please the mob and his fear of official censure if he failed in his duty to bring us safely to Kaoping. I then handed him little Hope to carry and there he was with the little girl held high before the people and the two ladies clinging to his gown on either side.

He made one further attempt to elude us when he handed Hope back to me. But I reminded him again of his solemn responsibility.

"Your duty is to take us to Kaoping. If we can't stay the night at Yincheng, you must take us elsewhere."

"How do you suppose that we are to get elsewhere?" he replied. "Our cart is away back at the inn."

"Very well," I said, "you have to get us all somehow to Kaoping, and your business is to send to the inn and have the cart brought here."

At this moment there appeared two soldiers in uniform, driving the crowd to right and left with their cudgels. They made their way to the officer and entered into conversation with him. We caught him once more trying to edge his way to the edge of the crowd to escape us as he kept on talking, but we frustrated him again.

The sun had set and the short twilight would soon be merging into darkness. Who could tell what the rabble might do then? Instinctively we had felt that the crowd could not be restrained much longer. Marvellous indeed it was that they had been held in check even until now. But the arrival of the two soldiers, whatever the duty that brought them, certainly changed the temper of the crowd. It may be that, after conference with the officer, they went in and out among the people persuading them that we were being taken as Imperial prisoners to Kaoping where we were to be officially executed by order of the Empress.

As we prayed, I fear my faith was hardly prepared for the answer God vouchsafed to our prayers. The impossible to us was again proved to be possible for Him, as with wonder and thanksgiving, we saw the cart making its way through the dense crowd towards us. No need for the officer to tell us to mount. The sullen silence amid which we took our seats broke into a confused roar as we drove off. Once again we heard the now familiar cry "Death to the 'foreign devils'!" hurled after us as we bumped on our way out of Yincheng. In a few minutes the sounds grew faint and as darkness fell we were alone once more in the heavenly quiet of lonely roads.

CHAPTER FOURTEEN

THE OFFSCOURING OF ALL THINGS

OUR escort were in no mood either to talk themselves or to hear us talk, so that the way was pursued in silence. And indeed we were not sorry to have it so, for we were unspeakably weary. How long we had been travelling I do not know, but it must have been over an hour when we entered a moderate-sized village. The long narrow street was deserted and all was quiet as we pulled up before the dilapidated door of the only inn. We had to wait for the innkeeper to come out but when he saw that there was only a cart-load of "foreign devils" to cater for, he slammed the gate with a curse and bade us be gone.

Every bone in our bodies was aching with excessive weariness, until it had become almost unbearable under the harsh jolting of the springless cart. The thought of going any further was agony. Yet that is what our guards elected to do and for another hour or more we steeled ourselves to endure the unendurable. However, the quiet of the solitary roads, the freedom from mental strain, the cover of darkness that hid us from recognition and even the very fact that we were moving brought an element of comfort. It was, above all, a valued time for waiting on God to renew our strength for what was immediately before us.

We arrived at the next village, only to receive again at the only inn a rebuff similar to that which we had just experienced. We were tasting what it meant to be despised and rejected with our Master. Clearly there was nothing for it now but just to take what we could get and betake ourselves, like beggars, to the local temple. A few minutes later we were delivered at the theatre stage in front of the temple buildings. We were ordered to dismount, and the escort tethered the mule without taking him out of the shafts. Saying that they were going to negotiate a night's rest for us with the village elders inside, they disappeared behind the temple wall.

Believing that their reappearance was but a matter of a few minutes, we looked around to see where we might sit down. Our forlorn little group, the children fast asleep, was soon sitting uncomfortably on a pile of stones. Nor were we unnoticed by the few loungers still about. The word went round that there were "foreign devils" in the village and a little crowd quickly gathered, filled with the same hatred and murderous thoughts as others we had faced.

Taken up with the attitude of the crowd, my thoughts were not on the cart. Suddenly a cry from my wife startled me to my senses: "Quick, Archie, quick! they are bolting!" Sure enough they were. Seeing us surrounded by people the escort thought they saw their opportunity and untethered the mule without our noticing. My wife just caught sight of them as they dashed past and were away. Quick as thought I was on my feet and after them. All sense of weariness was gone. I flew as on wings. The mule was a spirited animal and making the pace under the driver's lash, but I got him before he was half-way down the street. Gripping the reins at the bit, I held him until my wife and Miss Gates, who were following behind with the children, caught up with me. The escort were furious but excused themselves by saying that they were just taking the animal to its night's stabling!

"Very well; then you take us with him," we said. And we clambered on board, to their great disgust.

But as we proceeded, we found that we were retracing our steps and hastening back towards Yincheng. We immediately told the escort that we would not think of going back to either Yincheng or Wangfang where our reappearance would endanger our lives. But the only answer was a storm of abuse. My heart quailed under it, for it seemed now as if they had reached the point where they could no longer tolerate our presence.

As we drew near to Yincheng again and heard, late as it was, the distant roar of riotous revel still going on in the town, I said to the officer in courteous tones:

"We are not willing to enter the town. You know they wanted to put us to death there and you are not wise in risking death for us again. We trust you to find us a suitable lodging elsewhere."

"We are going nowhere else tonight," he said fiercely. "Where should I find stabling at this hour if not at Yincheng? If you don't wish to come, get out and sleep under the hedge. You slept out last night, and you can do it again tonight."

I thought they were about to abandon us by the wayside. But after a consultation out of our hearing, the officer left one soldier in charge of us and went off on his horse with the other. Soon some of the revellers began to go home and as they passed the stationary cart in the middle of the road there were the usual questions: "Who have you got there?" "The cursed 'foreign devils'," came the answer and that was a signal for the questioners to join the escort in heaping scurrilous abuse on us. But no one raised a hand against us.

The suspense was ended by the return of the other two. The officer's manner seemed to indicate that he had urgent business on hand. After a few words, which we could not catch, to the group around us, he gave an order to proceed into Yincheng. It was after midnight when we reached the city gate and re-entered the place of former sorrows. Instead of taking us to a respectable inn, the escort stopped the cart inside the gate and ordered us to get out. The place indicated to us as our resting place for the night was the stage of the stone theatre, open to the four winds and facing directly on to the main street. Such places are the customary sleeping ground of tramps, outcasts and professional beggars. It was evident to us all that we had no choice but to accept this cheerless lodging. With heavy hearts we mounted to the stage by a steep stairway of small narrow steps, but not before receiving the solemn assurance that the escort would call for us at dawn the next morning, before the town was astir.

Happily for us the darkness hid from sight the horrible filth amid which we were to lie. Nothing was discernible save the dark forms of some five others, beggars and outcasts like ourselves, stretched in the attitude of sleep. The officer woke up one of these and told her—for this was a woman—to watch us carefully till the morning when we were to die and on no account allow us to escape. Then, throwing us three or four small steamed bread rolls, he jumped on the cart and was gone.

The old woman, in whose charge we had been left, affected no small solicitude for us. She mourned our plight, deplored the fate that awaited us the next day and then urged us to lay ourselves down to sleep beside the rest of her gang. When she found that we preferred to withdraw to the opposite corner and into the deepest shadows, she came and settled herself beside us, watching us intently, and giving vent to her inner feelings in a series of sighs, mutterings and ejaculations. It was a dreary business listening to a voice in the dark, with its hoarse, low monotone, "Ay-ya! ay-ya! they are all to be killed in the morning!" The consciousness of being thus closely overlooked by a hag who, for aught we knew, had a stake in our destruction, was disturbing enough to make sleep out of the question. How much the poor old soul took in of the Gospel message, lovingly given by Miss Gates, it is impossible to say. But it was not reassuring to see her, after supposing that we were asleep, steal away to her four male companions, softly arouse them and sit talking with them for a while before resuming her moanings beside us.

The sound of Miss Gates' voice bidding her go and rest in her own place took them all by surprise and she quietly obeyed. How we managed to keep awake that night I really do not know, but the situation demanded it. We took short watches in turn, though the snatches of sleep thus afforded were but troubled nightmares. Our nerves were on edge and fears of every sort filled our weary minds.

The break of day brought home to us the full indignity of our position. As my eye turned from my beggar associates in all their filth and squalor to the forms of my wife and children beside me and saw them where they lay, my heart bled at the sight. To any passer-by we must have looked, in our rags and dirt, as one company with the rest. And yet with it we had the sweetest solace in the knowledge that unto us it was being given in the behalf of Christ to suffer for His sake. Many times in the course of our sad journeyings some moment of peculiar darkness would be shot through with heavenly light by a word from the lips of our children, uttered in all the simplicity of childlike innocence and trust. There was one such moment now. The sorrow of seeing their outward wretchedness led to the following conversation:

"Father, dear!" said Hedley.

"What is it, darling boy?"

"I think Jesus must have slept in a place like this, when He had nowhere to go!"

"Yes, darling, very likely!"

"Then we ought to be glad that we are like Jesus, oughtn't we?"

The beggars were astir with the dawn. For a while they sat over a fire of sticks talking together and eyeing us askance. An early opened food shop close by supplied them with a meal. Then with broad daylight they decamped, as if fearful of us and glad to get away from our presence, the old woman among them. Her trust had been fulfilled. But there was no sign of our escort. The promised time of dawn had gone by and no cart appeared. Dawn melted into clear daylight and daylight into the brilliance of cloudless sunshine; and still no cart came. In another hour or so, the town would be astir and our presence known. What should we do? Flight would be madness. Sitting still was madness. Eventually we were all brought to one mind in the matter; and we resolved to remain where the will of God had placed us.

In due time the usual signs of awakening life appeared and the ones and twos that came down the street stopped to look at the sight of the strange group against the wall of the stage. Curiosity brought some of them up for a closer look. The attentions of the crowd soon became so offensive that we were forced to leave the stage for the street where we sat down on some wayside stones. There we sat until the hot sunshine and the crowd milling around us drove us back to the shelter of the stage.

There were a number of instances of individuals showing us kindness during our sorrowful journey and there was one now. Our clothes were still badly torn and Miss Gates appealed to one old woman for the loan of a needle and thread. The dear old soul readily complied and the rents were repaired.

And still the escort failed to put in an appearance. The long hours went by. At last, the state of exhaustion to which we were being reduced by hunger and thirst forced me to crave a little water from the food shop hard by. In the compassionate mercy of God the request was not denied and I had the joy of reappearing with a bowl of hot water in each hand. Not only so but the innkeeper repeated this kindness until our thirst was satisfied. The Lord remember those cups of water given us at a time when to befriend the foreigner was to court the foreigner's doom!

It was going on for noon now and still there was no sign of the cart that had been promised for dawn. But the comfort was ours that we were in the appointed place of

God's providence and our hearts were in peace because we trusted Him. Suddenly we experienced the bounding joy of the sight which at length rewarded our faith—the officer with his long pipe hurrying past on foot! He paused for a moment to tell us in an offhand way that they were soon coming to take us on; then tossing us some more steamed bread, he hastened away. Here at last was a double mercy—the certainty that the escort had not deserted us and the supply of our need of food. Out of a full heart we gave thanks to Him whose mercy endureth for ever.

CHAPTER FIFTEEN

A DAY OF DARKNESS

ABOUT noon two horse soldiers with drawn swords passed out of the town by the gate close to us and we were informed that they were our executioners with orders to await our coming and despatch us by the way. Thus our minds were directed perpetually to the thought of death rather than deliverance. The cherished hope that the cart had been given us for life died within us and in its place there was another hope—that in nothing we should be ashamed, but that with all boldness Christ might now be magnified in our body by death, since the will of God was so.

About half an hour later the officer reappeared and ordered us to follow him outside the gate. Two carts were awaiting us instead of one. But instead of the comparatively comfortable passenger cart in which we had hitherto been travelling, there were now two low coal trolleys, common in those parts, with solid wheels of small diameter. This type of cart is locally known as the "mountain tiger" from the facility with which it traverses the steep and narrow passes with its load of coal. The body of the cart is simply a strong wooden frame—nothing else: no side supports, no awning overhead and nothing beneath to break the concussion.

The ladies and children were ordered to seat themselves on the one, while I was to follow alone on the other. What else could this mean than that we were common felons, riding to a felon's death? In silence we set out for a second time from Yincheng. There was no hostile demonstration like that of the day before. The crowd watched us out of sight with scarcely a word spoken.

Separated now from the fellowship of my companions I was left to my own reflections. The bitterness of that lonely ride who can tell? Some may perhaps wonder why, after such signal deliverances and sustaining grace, faith did not rise superior to the new trial. I only record the fact that it was so. Seasons of darkness do not necessarily argue the failure of faith. Often the very reverse. For faith needs to be educated and its schooling has to be done in the valley of sorrow as well as on the hill of vision. There was, in any case, a good deal to account for the mood from the physical side alone. It was now a month since we had first taken the road. The hope of deliverance which had buoyed us up was failing. Then there was the thought of what my dear wife was enduring on that barbarous trolley under the scorching blaze of the noonday sun. I had represented to the officer that, in my wife's condition, such a mode of conveyance was the refinement of cruelty. But the only answer was a callous "It can't be helped. There's nothing better!"

At the boundary where the Kaoping jurisdiction commenced, we were halted before a small yamen from which the official emerged carrying two small pennons of Imperial yellow, each inscribed with four characters "Officially forwarded by the Luan district magistrate". These he carefully affixed with his own hands to the harness of the mules in each cart and gave the signal to move on. It seemed to me that those yellow symbols could represent only one thing—our death warrant.

Some little time after, however, as I sat praying and reminding God of the mighty deliverances He had already wrought for us, the thought flashed into my mind as a revelation that the flags were the symbols of Imperial protection. And God used this thought to bring back to my heart the hope I had lost and to strengthen my hold of Him as the "Mighty to save". I jumped off the cart and ran ahead to share my new confidence with the others and as I did so the words of the promise given to my wife on the morning of flight, "I shall not die, but live, and declare the works of the Lord", revived in our hearts to the quickening of our faith.

As we reached the summit of the pass and began to descend on the Kaoping side, the travelling became too awful for words. Our guards seemed to have lost sight of the fact that the trolleys were carrying human beings, not sacks of coal. They would probably have been more careful if the freight had been coal or iron instead of flesh and blood. What we were enduring was literal torture. The declivity became a succession of ledges, down which the "mountain tiger" plunged, leaping from one to the other with a recklessness all too cruelly facile. The jolt and bang of the earlier progress now gave way to a series of crashes, the concussion of which was alarming. Even the escort relaxed so far as to allow us to make the descent on foot. In this way we were brought once more together and under the burning sun we toiled down to the foot of the pass.

The scorching heat not only fell on us from above but

I

was refracted like a furnace from the rocks around. No refreshment either of food or drink was given us and our bones ached again with the severity of the ride. Yet dear little Hope sang to us happily as we went along.

All things have an end, even a never-ending twenty miles of jolt and crash and sweltering heat. At seven o'clock we entered the city. The two horse soldiers who had preceded us from Yincheng had not been encountered on the road and in all probability had been sent on to prepare the Kaoping magistrate for our coming.

As we entered the yamen enclosure the huge crowd pressed in with us. The trolley carts were driven away, the escort went to report and we were left standing alone in the thick of it. All attempts by the runners to quieten the people and keep them back were unavailing. With hoots and yells they thronged in upon us and forced us up the steps by the inner gate. The excitement grew in intensity and but for our timely admittance to the inner courtyard it must have gone hard with us. In the mercy of God, the gate opened just at the moment of our extremity and we were pulled inside and locked into a room containing two small *kangs*. Prison though it was, it seemed the calm of Paradise after the howling storm outside.

Once more God proved Himself better than our fears and magnified His name as the Lord merciful and gracious. An excellent supper of rice, bread and eggs was ordered for us by the Mandarin; and though he did not come to interview us himself he sent in his son to assure us that we were to be escorted to the next magistracy at Tsehchow in the morning. He kindly made us a gift of a thousand cash for the road. We were also visited by several minor officials and many of the gentry who plied us with questions of the usual curious sort without betraying sympathy or antipathy. There was one remarkable exception, however.

A gentleman of the yamen, looking hard at me, said:

"Surely you are one of the two missionaries who were over here about two months ago preaching in the south suburb?"

"Yes," I replied, "I am."

"The Jesus doctrine is a good doctrine and your words were very good. It is pitiable to see the honourable pastor in a beggar's rag. Will you please exchange it for this of mine?"

And he presented me with a gown of blue calico—one certainly that had been well worn, but which was still most presentable, and to my eyes a princely garment. This unexpected act of kindness was an indication that there might be others among them who at heart were well disposed towards us, little as they cared to show it. At any rate, the treatment we were receiving did not look like execution and the assurance given us that we should be sent on next day strengthened our belief that our life was not to be taken here at least.

Happily for us we were unaware that on that very day, at Taiyuan, the provincial capital, forty-four men, women and children were ruthlessly put to the sword. Earlier Yü-hsien, the governor, had issued an order that every foreigner in Shansi was to be sent up to Taiyuan for execution. Why, therefore, we were not sent north instead of south is a mystery. We might well have been among that company of martyrs. Our escape was all the more remarkable in that we were sent on under arrest with nothing but a criminal's passport and were therefore at the mercy of each Magistrate. None of them was bound to send us on, as they would have been if we had been travelling with a full safe-conduct pass. Thus we never knew when we left one city what awaited us in the next. More than once we were on the point of being sent back to Luan and once it was all but decided to send us direct to Yü-hsien himself. Of the nineteen yamen through which we passed, fourteen were so far anti-foreign that it was a moot point with each whether we should be passed on, sent back or executed there and then.

Unaware therefore of the dreadful events of that very day in the provincial capital, we stretched ourselves, at a late hour after all the visitors had left, on the stone bed and slept a sweet, restful sleep with one pillow between us —my beggar garment, which we rolled up and put under the children's heads.

On July 10th, at the break of day, we were knocked up and ordered hurriedly outside. An escort of six, four of whom were soldiers in uniform armed with bludgeons, was awaiting us. To my distress the two carts were the same coal trolleys of yesterday. I remonstrated and entreated them at least to give the ladies a litter; but the request was impatiently refused. There was no time now to think about a litter. If we did not wish to be attacked by the city mob we must be gone. And off they hustled without further ceremony.

That long, long stretch of thirty miles to Tsehchow is a terrible memory. The whole journey was a repetition of its predecessor—crash, crash over mountain roads and boulder-strewn passes. Throughout the entire day, with the exception of one hour at an inn, we were exposed to the full power of the sun, in the same unprotected condition as heretofore. But these were the least of our sufferings.

About 9 a.m., when we had made some ten miles, we drew near to a large market town. Before entering it the escort warned us that the folk were notoriously anti-foreign and that we should never get through. We had no sooner entered the gate than we were driven into an inn and taken as usual to a back room. Our little store of road money gave us a measure of independence and we had the satisfaction of buying our own food for the first time and also of investing in the luxury of a wooden comb.

Outside there was the usual rowdy and unruly mob and we could well believe that, but for the restraining hand of God, they would gladly have taken matters into their own hands and done what others had so far failed to do. Even the escort were surprised at our immunity from harm. The scraps of conversation which we overheard suggested that they were now intending to get rid of us in some way on the next stretch of the journey.

Resuming the journey, therefore, we were filled with much anxiety. But nothing happened to make us suspicious during the next three hours which brought us to another large village where we were driven to the farther end and halted before a small shrine. The animals were taken out and led to the refreshment of the inn; the guard betook themselves to food and rest. Only we were left, sitting on the trolleys in the scorching heat and exposed to the uncertain temper of an ever-growing crowd.

Back in the inn the escort were scheming against our

lives. Foreign blood must be spilt by reason of the drought. But the question was, how much? Should all the members of our party be put to death, or only one? And should the victim be a child or an adult? As reports of the discussion were whispered around in our hearing, there were many expressions of sorrow and sympathy. Finally, a message came through to the effect that it had been decided to put the ladies to death on the spot and to take on only the children and myself to Tsehchow. The reason for this seems to have been that foreign women were credited with possessing an evil influence of peculiar malignity and that to them the drought and other evils were mainly attributable.

What the agony of that message was to each one of us can only be known to God. As my beloved wife received it, the momentary spasm that shot across her face revealed the depth of the inward anguish, to be replaced immediately by the heavenly light I had seen once before when in the immediate presence of death. Turning to me she said, with unfaltering voice, "I do thank God that you and the children are to be spared. It is a comfort to me now that they will have you to care for them." But the thought of having first to witness and then to survive the murder of my wife was insupportable; and, for the dear children as for myself, I could not but desire of God the mercy of deliverance through death from such unspeakable sorrow.

As the escort emerged at last from the inn, followed by the mules, we knew that the critical moment had come. The animals were put in and the order to go was given. Amid a silence strangely like the hush that had prevailed when we left the morning inn, the trolleys moved forward. An awe that rooted them to the spot settled upon the crowd; and instead of being driven to yonder field at the right of the shrine, we passed on through the gate to the Tsehchow road. *At the last minute the decision had been reversed*—whether through the irresolution of the elders or some other cause matters not. That it was in no sense due to any change in the escort's disposition towards us was evident. They tried yet once again to get rid of us by sending on two of their number to the last place of any size before Tsehchow to incite the people to fall on us. But though a mob of several thousand was waiting for us, they fell back on either side as we passed through. The same mysterious hush we had known before was upon them as we slowly traversed the narrow path between the crowds; and to the unconcealed amazement of the disgusted soldiery not a soul broke bounds or gave heed to the summons to fall on us.

We arrived at last, faint and weary at the end of that terrible and wonderful journey, at Tsehchow. Hunger and thirst and aching limbs were forgotten in the realization of its threefold deliverance.

CHAPTER SIXTEEN

PERILS IN THE CITY

THE prefectural city of Tsehchow was traditionally anti-foreign. It is true that the Roman Catholics had succeeded in settling within its walls but visiting Protestant missionaries had more than once been driven from their inn and expelled from the city.

The sun was nearing the western horizon when we arrived at the great gate. No one can realize what it meant to face the thought of entering a hostile Chinese city. Villages and towns were trial enough but the mere sight of the battlemented walls towering high before us had a dread of its own. We had barely entered the gate when we were stopped by a party of yamen officials at the head of a waiting crowd, amongst whom we recognized the evil face of the foremost of our Hantien accusers. In the most violent and offensive way they seized the animals' heads and, forcing them round, ordered us to leave the city.

For several moments our fate hung in the balance, as they abusively refused to hear of our admittance. We therefore faced the alternative of being taken back to Kaoping or being turned adrift to tramp the roads. However, when the officer in charge produced the papers which he was deputed to carry to the sub-Prefect the situation immediately changed. The officials quickly ran over them and then gave orders to take us to the yamen.

If we ever needed to realize the encompassing of the

invisible host of God, it was in the streets of Tsehchow. The trolleys were followed by an ever-increasing and tumultuous mob, the dimensions of which, by the time we reached the yamen gates, were alarming enough. As we drove into the enclosure they thronged in after us and when, a moment later, we dismounted, we found ourselves, as at Kaoping, alone and unprotected in their midst, without even a "runner" to guard us. There was nothing for it but to stand where we were amid the scorn and buffetings of the wild mob and quietly wait to see what was to be done with us.

We had not long to wait. Fearing a riot within the yamen precincts, the Mandarin ordered us to be escorted off the place as if to abandon us to the violence of the mob. Foreseeing danger, I refused to go and demanded the right of a personal interview with the Mandarin. My request was answered with derisive laughter and my refusal to move with forcible ejection.

There followed a distressing experience when we were crushed by the thronging, struggling, yelling crowds up against the main gate where we had contrived to stay to avoid being swept into the open street. We had our work cut out to soothe the children and shield them from the pressure which at times almost crushed the breath out of us.

At last the Mandarin's deputies appeared, to announce that we were to be lodged for the night in an inn on the street. We were to be sent on the next day to Hwaiching. I remonstrated again, for the prospect of a night in an inn under these circumstances was terrifying. But in vain. So we were taken to an inn in the principal thoroughfare and shown to our room in a tiny courtyard, where a single representative of the yamen was left to "guard" us. For the next few hours we were "made a spectacle unto men". At first Miss Gates and I tried to protect my wife and the children by allowing the crowd to see and question us at the door of the room. But finally, the pressure forced us in and the room itself was jammed with people. Apart from the vicious attitude of those who were watching us, the heat and the stench were overpowering, the cravings of hunger and thirst intense, and head and limbs and every bone aching again with the hardships we had already endured.

Not until a late hour did the crowds withdraw, leaving just the half-naked yamen underling lying in a room at the other side of the yard, placidly fusing the opium pill over the lamp flame. When all was quiet and the shop door barred, I made my way to the innkeeper and ordered food. Several previous attempts to do so had failed and now again he refused to cook for us. So we had to make shift with the dregs of the copper in which the evening millet had been boiled.

I fully intended to keep watch during the night while the others slept, but alas for resolutions, even under circumstances of such grave peril! I fell into a deep sleep from which I did not awake until daybreak, only to learn that I had slept through hours of battering at the gate and a wild pandemonium which sounded as if all hell had been let loose.

It was not till afterwards that we learned how gravely critical the situation had been. At midnight the whole city was in riot. With horrible cries and yells they rushed to the Roman Catholic mission first and fired the premises, the priests barely escaping with their lives. Then they came to our inn and howled for us to be brought out to them. How they came to disperse without having their wish gratified we could never learn. I only know that when I awoke it was as quiet as when I lay down. The fact is all the more remarkable when it is considered that not two days later our sister, Miss Rice, of the Lucheng party, was brutally done to death not far from the walls of this very city.

It was still early when a petty official from the yamen entered with an underling and half a dozen soldiers and ordered us out. We were to start our onward journey to Hwaiching immediately to prevent further rioting. We were told that the only conveyance provided was to be three donkeys. My dismay was all the greater when the animals arrived carrying only the bare wooden frames with which pack animals are saddled for the transport of merchandise. We were expected to travel thirty miles in this manner!

"This is preposterous!" I said. "We refuse to move till you have brought us two mule litters!"

A lively demonstration followed. But I held my ground, though I am bound to say I was amazed when they eventually took two of the three donkeys back and returned in half an hour with a single mule litter for the women and children. It was really only an apology for a litter, consisting of bare poles and nothing to cover the rope mesh but a fragment of an old straw mat, dirty and frayed. There was not even a canopy of any kind for privacy and shade. But further bargaining was impossible and I accepted the inevitable with as gracious a "Thank you" as possible.

It was pitiful to see the crushed, constrained position of the four in the litter. My wife and Miss Gates faced each other with their backs against the poles and between them, in a space hardly big enough for their legs, the two children were somehow jammed in. They were hoisted to the mules' backs and I mounted the saddle-rack provided for my torture and we were off. There was the usual excited crowd to escort us away in the belief that we were being taken to our execution.

The prospect of another day under the burning sun without any protection was full of dread. It is true that we now had a little money, but, as condemned prisoners, we were not allowed to buy for ourselves. We were therefore compelled to hand over some of the money to the underling for the purchase of hats and fans. The rascal returned with five tiny rush fans of the cheapest kind and the ready lie that there were no hats to be bought. He chuckled as he slung his own cash bag over his shoulder, the heavier by several hundreds of our cash.

When travelling by day we could never count upon being free from a crowd of some kind, even in secluded spots. They seemed to spring from nowhere, where but a moment before we were alone. And so, all the morning long, our ears were regaled with the refrain of the current Boxer song. Each passer-by would ask the stock question:

"Where are you from?"

"Tsehchow!" the muleteer answered.

"Whom have you got there?"

"Foreign devils!"

"Where are you taking them to?"

"To death at Hwaiching!"

Then would follow the terrible refrain again:

> The wrath of the gods
> For vengeance doth call;
> *Foreign blood must be spilt*
> Ere the rain can fall.

As the day advanced and the power of the sun increased, we suffered greatly: the heat and the flies were terrible and the fans were scarely any protection. The ladies and the children endured intense discomfort in their cramped positions in the litter. To make matters worse, my wife was now suffering from dysentery. The children frequently sobbed uncontrollably from the smart of the raw blisters caused by sunburn on their arms and legs. Even the underling was moved enough to loan my wife his broad-brimmed straw hat and to allow me to pluck leafy branches from the wayside trees with which to cover the children's blistering legs.

About noon we asked when we were to stop for the midday halt and meal. But the escort's reply was quite non-committal. In sorrowful silence we journeyed on over the rugged mountain road. At length we were halted in the narrow side-street of a small village, before a crazy-looking hovel where the mules were taken out to be fed. A poor miserable looking woman, the occupant of the hovel, was told to look after us. Thankful for any shelter from the awful blaze, we followed her inside. Her pitiable poverty revealed itself, not only in the condition of the house, but more than all in the pinched and sorrowful face. The circumstance of suffering common to us all

seemed to draw her to us, and later on, when the guards
were out of earshot, she expressed a very touching sympathy with us in the knowledge of our impending execution. Then she poured out the heart-rending tale of the
general distress as the result of the long drought. It was a
God-given opportunity for the Gospel message and the
dear woman's heart seemed ripe to receive it. All the
hunger and the thirst were forgotten in the deep joy of
ministering the word of life to that needy soul and our own
sorrows were swallowed up in the consolation of pointing
a weary and heavy-laden one to the Saviour of whom
she had never yet heard. There was a radiance on the
sisters' faces as they told me about it.

Soon the journey was resumed. The muleteer was hard
and cruel to a degree in his lack of sympathy for the
passengers in his litter. I myself, unable to endure the
galling of the pack-saddle, had been walking barefoot
almost continuously since we left Tsehchow. Once I asked
the soldier escort if I might take a turn on his comfortable
saddle while he was stretching his limbs by walking. The
request was treated with contemptuous silence. It was
escorts like this who were responsible for the murders of
not a few of our Shansi brethren and sisters and I have
often wondered that we ourselves came out alive from
under the hands of such men.

We were now in the border country between Shansi
and Honan and were still of the belief that once we were
out of Shansi, our dangers would be much less. So far as
we knew the Boxer movement had not spread to Honan
and there was an unutterable longing to be clear of the
province whose name was now a synonym for terror.

CHAPTER SEVENTEEN

ABUNDANCE OF RAIN

WE had not been on the road more than a couple of hours after the midday halt, when we arrived at a large town called Lanchen high in the hills near the border of the province. To my surprise and concern, instead of pressing on towards Hwaiching, we were halted, the litter set down in the street and its occupants turned out. We had reached the border control office and from the building opposite two men came out to examine the papers presented by the Tsehchow yamen representative.

"What's this? These papers are irregular!" we heard them say as they took them inside for more careful scrutiny: "This is not a regular safe-conduct pass!"

From what we overheard of the conversation inside, this meant detention at least—and just when we were almost over the Shansi border! I was hardly prepared, however, for what happened next. We were ordered into the room, while the escort charged with taking us to Hwaiching calmly led out our animals and took the road back to Tsehchow! Five men mounted guard over us and all our movements were closely watched. When the inevitable crowd collected, the guards ordered us outside and we sat on the doorstep until dark. Under pretext of putting the children to bed, my wife was able to withdraw while Miss Gates and I continued to satisfy the general curiosity. At last we were locked into the room with the guard of five men.

It was an intensely hot midsummer night. The room, in size about twenty feet by twelve, was very low and in a filthy condition. Ventilation there was none except that provided by the finger-made holes punctured in the paper window. The door was fast barred and locked. The fire, which had been in use all day for cooking, was kept in all night: and ten persons were in the room! Moreover, the atmosphere reeked with the sickly fumes of opium and tobacco, blown from the pipes of the five gaolers, whose forms were revealed by the opium lamp, lying stark naked around us. To add to these miseries the *kang* was infested with bugs, whose depredations were reinforced by the attacks of mosquitoes.

Outside, the mob howled for our death until a late hour of the night, then went home for a while. But at daybreak the crowds began to reassemble, demanding the execution of the death sentence. We were facing a new and perhaps our last crisis. Nothing but the intervention of God could deliver us. At this moment the promise was borne in upon me powerfully, "Call upon Me in the day of trouble; I will deliver thee, and thou shalt glorify me." My faith was strengthened to lay hold of it and to plead it with God *for the present hour* of our trouble. Our part was to call upon Him; and realizing that the cause of their rage against us was the continued drought, we were moved to make a united cry to God to intervene on our behalf by sending rain enough to satisfy the need of these poor sufferers and because of our extremity to send it now. Accordingly, kneeling up on the bed we poured out our hearts before Him in Chinese so that the gaolers might know exactly what we were doing and what we were asking.

How long we continued in prayer, I cannot tell. I only know that scarcely had we risen from our knees when the windows of heaven were opened and down upon the howling mob swept the sudden fury of a torrential flood of waters. In a few seconds the street was deserted and not a sound was heard but the swish of the rushing rain.

The effect upon our gaolers was immediate: something akin to awe took the place of their hard incredulity and though they still affected a rough indifference towards us, they relaxed a good deal from the severity of the previous day. Whereas we had experienced the greatest difficulty in getting them to give us food at all, even at their own price, we were now supplied with a fair liberality, though not to the point of satisfaction. The door, too, was thrown open and we were allowed to stand at the threshold and drink in the sweetness of the rain-drenched atmosphere.

As the children and I stood at the inn door watching the swift rush of water as it ran down the street in a veritable river, we sang a chorus the children knew in Chinese:

> Praise, praise the Lord Jesus,
> Who gave His life for the world,
> And who rose from the dead.
> Praise be to Jesus, the Lord of grace.

As we sang, the talk in the room subsided. Our keepers were listening intently over their pipes and presently one was heard saying to the rest:

"They are praying to their God to send the rain faster

K

and just look!—it is actually coming down faster!"

The rain fell in sheets as though some mighty reservoir had suddenly burst its banks. Never have I seen such rain. All that day and far into the night it poured and poured, with a greater or lesser degree of intensity, and never stopped. Blessed be God! This was the "deep downpour" which alone could have satisfied the farmers.

With the people driven off the streets, we had a day of quietness and comparative privacy. The unusual monotony of an undisturbed morning was broken by the arrival of a courier from the Tsehchow yamen bearing a message for the gaolers. The rest of the day went quietly by until, about dusk, two men arrived. In spite of their bedraggled garments and generally woebegone appearance, their bearing betrayed the fact that they were gentlemen of the yamen—officials. They were evidently expected and were soon deep in conversation with the officer-in-charge. The subject under discussion was our death and the manner of it, as far as Miss Gates could gather.

We retired to the seclusion of the *kang* to face the end, as so often before, in the presence of God. Then, with the same calmness and composure as though she were in her own home, my wife prepared the children for bed. Laying them down, we sang with them their evening hymn.

"Sun of my soul, Thou Saviour dear!"

It was specially moving to hear their little voices in the words
"Be near to bless us when we wake",
and to know, as they did not, what the waking should bring.

When darkness set in, the door was barred and locked as before. The night air, charged with moisture, was heavy with a steamy heat. Shut in as we were under the same foul conditions as had prevailed the night before, the atmosphere of the room quickly became insufferable. In the midst of all these discomforts we set ourselves to watch and pray. As we reviewed the marvellous lovingkindness of that wonderful day, our hearts were drawn out in extolling the God of our salvation. We then proceeded to pray audibly in Chinese, so that the gaolers could hear and understand, for the direct intervention of God to bring about our deliverance from the death immediately before us.

There was dead silence as the prayer went up. By the dull light of an opium lamp, we could discern the forms of the five men lying or sitting in different postures about the room; though we could not see the expressions on their faces. Presently, however, the silence was broken and out of the semi-darkness came the words:

"They have been praying to their God to deliver them. Ai-ya! deliver them indeed! Too late for that now. What is the use of praying when everything is fixed?"

It must have been shortly after midnight, as nearly as we could judge, when a stealthy knock was heard at the door and a voice demanding admittance. The bolt was thrown back, the bar drawn and the silhouette of one of the Tsehchow officials appeared in the doorway.

"Up, up!" he said, to the gaolers, "up and be doing! Now's your time. These 'foreign devils' are in your power and you must put them to death. Do it any way you choose, but do it you must and do it now! Kill them at once and don't be afraid. Poison them with opium, if you like; and to prevent trouble, stupefy them first by burning such and such a narcotic. Do as I say and never fear!"

And with that he passed out into the darkness. The burden of this terrible communication was interpreted to me by Miss Gates in the whispered words:

"The end has come. The official has instructed them to kill us now."

Without giving the gaolers the slightest intimation that we had understood what had passed, we made our prayer to God and set a watch against them. The door was once more secured and a short consultation held; after which the men lay down again. In a little while they were, to all appearance, asleep. . . .

Time went on and we saw no indication that foul play was intended. Miss Gates was reclining in a half-sitting posture towards the back of the *kang*, veiled in shadow, which the yellow glimmer of the opium lamp failed to penetrate; while my wife and children were covered by my kneeling form as I swept the fan above them.

Then, very quietly, one of the men got up and busied himself with preparing some stuff in a vessel. When ready, he put a light to it and returned to his place. Soon after I began to feel very drowsy and I had to fight against a stupor which was driving me into unconsciousness. The noxious fumes of the burning drug were doing their work entirely to the satisfaction of the watching gaoler. Everyone, apparently, was in a deep sleep. He brought the lamp across to scrutinize his victims to see if the time had come to give the finishing stroke. What was his amazement to find, as he held the light to Miss Gates' face, that she was wide awake and that upon one of the "foreign devils" at least the narcotic had no effect.

"Ai-ya! not asleep yet? The bugs are too lively for you tonight, eh?"

He withdrew to the solace of his pipe, while our dear sister continued her lonely vigil of self-denying love and unceasing prayer to which we undoubtedly owed our lives.

It was still dark when I was startled out of my heavy torpor by cries and groans beside me. I sprang up to find my beloved Flora lying in Miss Gates' arms in the throes of asphyxiation. She was gasping, panting, struggling for breath and moaning for air. I turned to the gaolers and besought them to have pity on my dying wife and open the door, if only for one minute. The request was refused with a curse. What else could I expect, since her death was the very thing they were aiming at?

All that I had at my disposal was two tiny rush fans and with one in each hand I began to ply them as vigorously as I could, pleading my wife's promise "I shall not die, but live, and declare the works of the Lord". As the morning broke we had the unspeakable joy of seeing her breathing naturally and quietly again—prostrate in body, but rejoicing in spirit, giving glory to God.

Meanwhile the men made no move. The sun came up and the early clatter of hoofs told us that the busy traffic of the day had begun. At last the gaolers arose and dressed and we heard them discussing the events of the night and the answer they would make to the remonstrances of the official. They would say:

"These people have been praying to God, and we could do nothing against their prayers."

In due time the door was unlocked and thrown wide open and into the noisome prison room streamed the blessed light and air of heaven. Wonderful to say no exception was taken to our standing or even sitting in the doorway—a mercy for which we thanked God. The sweet freshness of the early morning was life to my wife in her exhausted state. The rain had ceased before day-break; and now there was a crisp, delicious coolness in the air which revived her like a strong tonic.

With the fall of rain, the people had for the time being forgotten us and in their eagerness to plant their autumn crops had scattered to the fields. As for the two officials from Tsehchow, we never saw them again. Their disappearance seemed to disrupt the councils of the gaolers who engaged in a lively argument about what to do with us now. Some were for carrying out the sentence as originally planned, others were for sending us forward and shifting the responsibility for our death on to the shoulders of the next Prefect.

The question was settled in a most unexpected way. Who should appear on the scene but the muleteer who had brought us here and who, we supposed, had returned to Tsehchow with the traitorous escort. Brutal as his attitude had formerly been, he now espoused our cause and with that reckless air and defiant look of his said:

"I care not a straw for your talk. My orders are to carry the 'foreign devils' to Hwaiching and to Hwaiching I carry them. If you put them to death here, you will be fools. Don't you know that all the fords of the Yellow River are held by the Big Sword Society and they will get no farther than the river? There is a band of them not far away and the devils may never reach the river."

Upon this he walked over to the other side of the road and dragged from a shed the framework of the litter and set to work upon the lashings. From that moment everything was done to hasten our departure. Three of the men from the Customs station accompanied us as escort, our papers were endorsed and given into the hands of the officer-in-charge and the necessary animals commandeered "for yamen use" from a passing convoy of coal carts. As I watched the men hoist the litter to the mules' backs, I could hardly believe my eyes. No crowds followed us— they were too busy in the fields. No insults were shouted after us. Instead of being carried out tumultuously to die outside the gate, we were journeying quietly to our destination, set forward on our way by the very men who until then had sought our lives.

CHAPTER EIGHTEEN

A GLEAM OF HOPE

FRIDAY, July 13th, was the eighth day of our second flight from Luan and the week seemed like a year, so much had been crowded into it of misery and suspense. But now we were on our way out of Shansi and the road lay through magnificent scenery, over the great stone stairway of the lofty Taihang range that divides the provinces of Shansi and Honan. The immemorial traffic of the great trade route has worn the rocky steep into a series of steps, so regularly graded that one wonders whether skilled labour has not been employed upon them. The pass is a nearly continuous ascent between rugged and precipitous rocks until an altitude of at least 5,000 feet above sea level is reached. Then it drops to the plains of Honan.

We revelled in the beauty of God's handiwork. Not that we were free—and neither driver nor escort had abated one jot of their rooted enmity towards us. Nor were the conditions of travel less rigorous than before. The heat and discomfort were just the same. Fortunately we had been able to procure pieces of cloth to cover the children's heads and these I kept moistening in the pools by the way. I myself was driven to walk and I was glad of the calico socks that had been left to me at Shahokou and the single Chinese style cloth shoe. This I wore on each foot alternately and eased the soreness by dipping my feet in the now frequent pools in the rocks.

As the litter swung over the irregular ground, it began bit by bit to disintegrate and my wife found herself sinking through the rope meshes and so incommoding the mule who began to kick. But the muleteer refused to stop to tighten the cordage until the usual halting place had been reached.

The sun was at its hottest when, to our great relief, we crossed the long-looked-for boundary line and felt ourselves to be beyond Yü-hsien's power. Yes, we were actually in Honan and had begun the descent to the green plains spread out below. In an hour or two we were travelling through the verdant rice-fields of Honan.

Soon we entered a large market town, notoriously anti-foreign, in the main thoroughfare of which we were halted. The mules were taken out and the litter frame set down—not in an inn, but in the street, which was inches deep in mud after the rains. Our arrival was the signal for a rush from all sides and we were at once hemmed in by a crowd. The escort and the driver had betaken themselves to the comfort and quiet of an inn, while we were told that if we wanted food we must go to the south suburb for it.

It was then that the dreaded words "Big Sword Society" grated on our ears again and shook our hearts. Several of the better disposed in the crowd warned us not to adventure ourselves into the south suburb, "as a detachment of the 'Big Sword Society' was there". So there were Boxers in Honan too! The truth filled us with dismay!

Faint and weary, we sought shelter from the scorching blaze and the oppressive crush under the awning of a

small bread shop near by where we hoped to get something to eat. When the shopkeeper refused to sell to us,
the ladies and the children were forced back to the
cramped discomfort of the litter in sheer self-defence.

For three hours we were beset by the crowds, never
knowing when we might be attacked. I dared not desert
the others to go in search of food. Standing or sitting
there, in or by the litter, in the open sun, and crushed on
all sides by the struggling, pushing throng was terribly
exhausting. The children kept sobbing with hunger,
terror, heat, sores and utter weariness after the long
journey. My dear wife, overcome by her great fatigues,
fell into a kind of swoon where she sat. Head and back
being unsupported, she fell heavily sideways and struck
her head violently against one of the poles. The blow
recalled her to the world of consciousness.

Now and again a hawker of viands or fruits would come
our way; but none would sell to us. At last one man was
induced to part with a few plums for an exorbitant
price, but a bid for a second instalment was refused.
Perhaps it was as well for us, ravenous though we were;
for they were but half ripe.

As time went on, we began to notice those signs in the
crowd which we had found from experience were precur-
sors of mischief. Noise and jostling were now the order of
the day and a spirit of open hostility began to manifest
itself. The opprobrious term "foreign devil" was used
more freely and coarse jests were flung at us. Under the
pressure, the poles of the litter were creaking ominously
and if once the framework gave way, it might well be
followed by its complete demolition and our destruction.

A feeling the nearest to panic that I had yet experienced came over me as I looked anxiously in the direction of the escort's inn. Just at the very crisis of our great need, the driver appeared with the mules, followed by the escort. The crowd fell back, the animals stood, the litter was hoisted and we were moving through their midst towards Hwaiching.

The roads were indescribably awful. Where they were not actually rivers, they were quagmires, through which I floundered wearily. I had to give up trying to wear a shoe and made the rest of the journey in bare feet. Where the mud or the water was too deep, I took to the saddle, however uncomfortable. And on these occasions I often became separated from the others in the litter. On one occasion I temporarily lost sight of them completely, to my intense alarm.

At last we reached the outskirts of Hwaiching and a sorry spectacle we must have presented to the crowd that thronged us as we passed along the street. We were taken to the sub-Prefect's yamen and put down in the inner courtyard just inside the gate. We were expected and soldiers and runners were there to keep back the mob. Not only so but the Prefect's palanquin was set there in evident readiness for immediate use. Almost before we had time to realize where we were, the cries of the runners to clear the road announced the coming of the Great Man, who hastily took his seat and was lifted to the shoulders of the bearers. The boom of the great gong that preceded him and the shouts of the underlings opened a way for the procession through the dense mass about us, and past us swept his lordship without deigning to lift his eyes. The next moment we were drawn into the vortex of soldiers and vassals who brought up the rear and ordered to "follow the chair" on foot.

To "follow the chair" was normally an insult of the most flagrant type. By the Mandarin's orders the ladies were compelled to take a place intended to brand them with shame, degradation and reproach—a place among the menials behind the chair, but in this case the intention was to secure our safety. To keep up with the Great Man's chair, borne by eight stalwart runners, was impossible, particularly in the exhausted state of the ladies, dragging along the children.

We must have traversed the city from one end to the other—so interminably long was the way—when we arrived at the place where the Great Man's chair had been set down. It proved to be the official inn reserved exclusively for yamen use. We were ordered to enter, the doors were shut and locked behind us and we were taken to a room which was comparatively clean, but absolutely destitute of furniture. There was not even so much as a straw mat to sit or lie on—nothing but the earth floor. A minute or two later a couple of chairs were brought in for our use and another placed in the courtyard opposite the door. On this His Excellency seated himself, surrounded by his retinue.

We were now ordered into his august presence; but as my wife was too exhausted to stand, she was allowed to remain seated at the door. As we presented ourselves before him he rose and remained standing throughout the short interview, in the course of which he asked us all about the journey, why we had left our station and where we were going. On hearing that we were making for Hankow, he remarked, "You are on a fool's errand, for you will never get there." And with a few instructions to those about him he haughtily took his departure.

The comparative kindliness of his manner was so unexpected after what we had hitherto experienced of official treatment that our hopes rose correspondingly and our spirits with them. The luxury of a place of refuge from the pressure of rude and hostile crowds and of leisure for undisturbed rest added to our peace of mind. And when at length a steaming hot savoury meal was brought in and set before us, it seemed no longer possible to doubt that we had fallen by God's mercy into good hands; and with fervent thanksgiving we blessed His holy name.

Having no definite clue, however, to the Mandarin's real intentions, we were not able to rid ourselves of those lurking fears which had by this time become a settled part of our constitution. Despite this we spent a good night. The lovingkindness of our God was manifested in many ways. For instance, the door of our room was not locked and, for the first time, we were allowed free access to the courtyard and the privy. Permission was also granted to take water for washing purposes from the water butt and two straw mats were handed to us for the women and children to lie on. We were glad to catch at every little thing that could be construed into an evidence of good will and were careful to express our gratitude to the guard.

With bricks for our own pillows and my beggar's garment as a pillow for the children, we soon fell asleep. The night passed uneventfully but for the challenge of the guard when I periodically got up to ease my aching limbs. The stars paled and slowly slipped from sight. The sky was once more reddening in the east and by sunrise the court-yard was a scene of animation. Two large Honan carts each hauled by three mules were in waiting and into these we were hastily thrust—the ladies and Hope in the first and Hedley and me following. Before the city was well awake, we were rumbling out of the great gate under a guard of eight soldiers with fixed bayonets, officered by the Mandarin's son himself on horseback, with a couple of mounted troopers to bring up the rear.

CHAPTER NINETEEN

EVIL TIDINGS

NOW began a series of fresh experiences in modes of travel which were to test our strength to the limit of endurance. For thirteen successive days we were to travel by cart and wheel-barrow, the suffering of which, in our condition, can only be described as torture. We were still treated as criminals and carried from place to place like ordinary felons.

As a result of all that we had passed through we had all lost a lot of weight, but especially my dear wife, suffering as she was from dysentery and the children with their wounds and excessive physical exhaustion. Yet day after day, for ten days, they were called upon to endure an average of ten hours on the bare floor of the springless cart as it rocked and jolted across country. We would start about 7 a.m. and not reach our day's destination till 7 p.m. or later. The only merit the carts had was that they were well covered in from the sun's fierce heat. But it is a miracle at which doctors marvel how any woman in my wife's condition could have survived such an ordeal.

On leaving Hwaiching, we struck due west, our course being in the direction of the city of Wuchih. The roads were largely under water and it was no uncommon thing for the cart to be axle deep in mud. Often it would tilt over to a dangerous angle, righting itself with a jolt. On one occasion at least, we stuck so fast in a bog that, for all the yelling and flogging and cursing, our three beasts could not haul the cart out until relieved of our weight.

At noon we were driven into the courtyard of a large village inn, wondering whether there would be a repetition of previous experiences. But the kindness and the attention of the Mandarin's son in command of our escort reassured us at once. While we enjoyed the handsome meal he ordered for us, he sat near the table, smoking his long pipe and chatting in the most affable way. The meal over, he took leave of us with a gracious bow and a gift of 1,500 cash. We did not see him again as he now returned home and left us in charge of the soldiers. Two hours of blessed rest were given us, when to stretch oneself full length on a bit of straw matting was the perfection of luxury. Then came the order to mount and we were off again, to the old tune of jolt and swing.

As we neared Wuchih, the soldiers again fixed bayonets, and, forming up on either side of the carts, took us as prisoners under arrest. It goes without saying that an immense concourse pursued us to the yamen gates and pressed in after us, where we dismounted amid the usual scenes of excitement. I had by now a nine days' growth of beard and wore a torn, bespattered gown and under my arm I was hugging the rolled up beggar's rag. The ladies' motley garments were soiled and torn and the children's combinations almost in tatters. On all of us were the marks of exposure, want and sorrow. No wonder we excited curiosity. But instead of the rest for which we yearned we had to face the noise and heat of jostling crowds and the ever present possibility of attack.

It was at Wuchih that we made our first acquaintance

with a real Chinese prison. We were taken to a small courtyard soon after arrival, and told to sit down on the narrowest of narrow benches against an outside wall. It was too uncomfortable and we preferred to stand. We soon tumbled to it that we were outside a cell for criminals. The clank of chains in the darkness betrayed the presence of some poor degraded creatures peering at us through the wooden bars of their prison cell. As we waited we wondered whether we too were about to join them as a prelude to the long-deferred execution.

After what seemed an interminable time, a messenger returned to take us into another courtyard. We were given a room to ourselves, but it was midnight before the crowd of attentive and friendly officials, with their interminable questions, left us to take our rest.

In the morning, the Mandarin himself was among our earliest visitors. When we heard that he was coming, we prepared to meet him appropriately. Runners cleared the way, a chair was set and a moment later we were face to face with the Great Man. He was very youthful looking and lacked the dignity of his Hwaiching colleague. As soon as he was seated, he addressed himself to us as to prisoners in loud, bullying tones, the offensiveness of which was possibly more apparent than real, while a retainer handed him his long tobacco pipe. With all his affected mannerism he was a friend to us, whether in his heart he wished us well or not.

It was at Wuchih that we gleaned our first tidings of the outside world and of the fearful trend of things in China itself. We were told that all the great powers were at war with China; that the foreigners had fled in confusion even

L

from Hankow and Shanghai and that there were now none left in the whole country. This threw light on the Hwaiching Prefect's enigmatical warning and made the chances of our getting through to our destination in peace and safety much slimmer.

We were also told of the awful tragedy at Paoting where the whole foreign community had been massacred, the women with great barbarity. This lent weight to the other reports. We were also warned that to go on towards Hankow via Nanyang would be very risky as several mission stations on the route had been rioted. It was even suggested that our only chance of getting safely to the coast lay in going due west into Shensi province and then south through Szechwan and Kweichow provinces. The futility of attempting such a journey was so apparent on the face of it that we had to take the risk of keeping to our present plans.

Further kindness was shown in the gift of some cast-off clothing for the children from the Mandarin's wife. Moreover there seemed to be a real spirit of inquiry towards the truth of God in Christ; and valuable opportunities were given, through the many questions pressed upon us, of preaching unto them Jesus.

The following morning, Sunday July, 15th, the carts were ready at an early hour to take us on another stage. The route chosen as likely to prove the least hostile was via Chengchow, Huchow and Sinyang. Breakfast was provided along with a little store of road money. We were now bound for the Yellow River and the county city of Yungchih on the other side.

Our soldier escort of six, however, was anything but

friendly. When I sought to speak to them of the grace of God, they turned on me fiercely with an order to desist, saying:

"Stop that talk! Don't you know that the Empress has made it a crime to preach the Jesus doctrine? Your Jesus has brought trouble enough to China; but China has finished with Him for ever."

Not far from the Yellow River we were halted at a quiet wayside hamlet, where we were mercifully free for once from crowds. The incident of our halt there, however, has survived in my memory not on this account, but because of a narrow escape from death at the hands of the escort.

"A few miles more and we shall be at the river," they said. "There are great dangers for you foreigners, and we can't guarantee to get you safely across unless you pay us for the trouble."

The dismay such a demand struck into us may be imagined, for we had to keep a jealous watch upon our tiny store of cash, as the margin for daily living was none too large. However, without betraying our inner feelings, we replied good-humouredly,

"Pay you for your trouble, good sirs? Why, it has nothing to do with us, as you know. This is a yamen matter; we are being forwarded by His Excellency of Wuchih, and he has made himself responsible for all payments by the way, your own included!"

"What the Master gives us won't nearly pay us for the risk we run. We must have so many hundred cash more per man or we can't do it."

Seeing that things were looking dangerous, I suggested

to Miss Gates meeting them half-way. But in deference to her wide experience in China, I gave way to her strong conviction that to yield at all would be fatal and would encourage them to rob us of everything. So we gave them a positive refusal to grant them a single cash. They gave us time to reflect on our mad decision, and then came back for the answer.

"Have you settled what you are going to give us?"

"We have told you once! We have little more than the necessary money for food and the matter of taking us arcoss the Yellow River is not our responsibility but the Mandarin's."

Abuse followed freely as they gave full vent to their rage. When this failed to make any impression, they turned to threats.

"Who but we can take you across in safety? Pay us the money we ask, or we will go back with the cart and leave you to find your way to Yungchih as best you can."

But by the mercy of God, they did not carry out their threats and we set off again. With mingled fear and joy we saw at length the turbid waves of the famous Hwang Ho (Yellow River) before us. How we got across God alone knows, because another attempt was made on the banks of the river to levy blackmail. When they found we were still adamant, they sat down to discuss what course to take. For hours our lives hung in the balance. I believe we were as near death then as ever we had been up to that time. The ferrymen too were in league with the soldiers.

At last the soldiers' irresolution whether to kill or spare us gave the ferrymen time to reconsider the advisability of securing a fare while they had the chance. And on the principle that half a loaf is better than none, they made a fresh advance. Whether the escort saw in this a welcome escape from an uncomfortable dilemma I cannot say. I only know that the bargain was concluded. Planks were laid to the boat and the carts rolled on board. The six mules were huddled into the well in the bows, the moorings were slipped, the sail hoisted and we were being borne swiftly down the current of the mighty river from death to life.

CHAPTER TWENTY

OUT OF DANGER

THE Yellow River crossing took three hours and was without noteworthy incident. Although there was nothing attractive about the monotonous mud banks of the wide, swift-flowing river yet the delight of that sail exceeded anything I had known on home waters, in more carefree days of the past. The luxury of water travel after the agony of the springless cart, the relaxation of spirit in the knowledge that another dreaded barrier would soon be past and our goal brought nearer and, above all, the deep, sweet peace of God, made the crossing a memorable experience.

We were not taken directly to the opposite bank, but to a landing place at some considerable distance downstream. Beyond a booth or two, the deep cart ruts up from the water's edge and a few riverside loafers, one would never have known it for a ferry terminus at all. As the boat drew in and touched bottom, it was to us as if we had reached the farther shore of the Red Sea, despite all the ugly rumours of the previous day.

An uncomfortable delay occurred, just at the moment when all was in readiness to resume the cart journey, due to a noisy demonstration by the boatmen who demanded their customary "wine money". Strictly speaking, we were prisoners under escort and it should have been the escort and not the prisoners to pay the money. But, thankful to be safely across the river, we agreed to pay the customary tip and everyone was satisfied. For the remainder of the journey to Yungchih, we travelled in peace.

On arrival we faced a grave period of suspense. The validity of our safe-conduct pass was called in question and the Mandarin debated whether to send us back across the river or not. Finally he decided to pass us on to the Chèngchow magistrate. At Chengchow, enormous crowds thronged about us to the yamen where we were dismounted in the courtyard and left to fend for ourselves. It was early afternoon and the sun was still hot. After being almost crushed in the swaying crowd for some time, the gate of the yamen opened and the Mandarin's deputy, holding our papers in his hand, ordered us inside.

The examination which followed with Miss Gates as spokesman was much like this:

"What country do you 'foreign devils' come from?"

"Our unworthy country is Great Britain."

"And how far off may that be?"

"Thirty thousand *li* by the sea route!"

"Ai-ya! You have not come all that distance to the Middle Kingdom for nothing. What are you here for?"

"Because we have been sent by the one living and true God, the Creator and Saviour of all men, to preach the glad tidings of His salvation for all men through the forgiveness of their sins."

"To be sure. Then you are Roman Catholics?"

"No. We have nothing whatever to do with the 'Lord of Heaven Church'. We belong to the 'Jesus Church'.[1] The two religions are separate and distinct."

[1] The names are thus distinguished in Chinese.

"Jesus Church? Jesus Church? . . . What else have you come for, besides preaching?"

"Nothing else at all!"

"Don't you tell me you are not here to make money out of us. What's your line of business?"

"We have no business. Our sole work is to persuade men to repent and turn to God from idols and to believe in Jesus Christ, His Son, who died for them and rose again."

"And pray, how long have you been in this country preaching this doctrine?"

Miss Gates answered for herself, "Fourteen years!" I answered for myself, "Three years!"

Fixing his eyes on my queue, he sneered:

"You only three years and grown all that hair? That's too good! Where have you been living in China?"

"In the province of Shansi, at the prefectural city of Luan."

"In Shansi, Luan, eh? And where are you going now?"

"Back to our own unworthy country, for the time being. We are now on the way to Hankow."

"Oh, yes, of course," he sneered again; "skulking out of the country. And for what reason, I should like to know?"

"It is not of our own wish that we are going. Your Honour knows well that we have no choice in the matter, owing to the disturbances created by the Big Sword Society."

The reference to the Boxers brought out his latent fury. Pointing to the papers that quivered in his hand and glaring with passion, he thundered:

"I'll tell you what you are. You are a parcel of runaways and you shall be dealt with accordingly."

This was an evident allusion to Yü-hsien's order that all foreigners resident in Shansi were to be forwarded direct to him at the provincial capital of Taiyuan, in accordance with the Imperial Edict issued for our extermination. The ominous manner of the man and his yet more ominous utterance could not fail to arouse the gravest apprehension for our safety. It seemed only too evident that we were in the hands of a Boxer official of the Yü-hsien type and there seemed to be a serious intention to send us back again to Shansi.

He had scarcely got his last words out of his mouth than the Mandarin himself arrived. There followed one of the most extraordinary and shameful scenes in all our varied experience. In the fever of his passion the Great Man had not taken the trouble to robe. He hurried on to the platform bareheaded and struggling into a soiled gown.

From the moment of his appearance, his mouth was filled with cursing and bitterness, launched against us with all the vehemence of frenzy. Pacing the platform like one possessed, he stormed and raved hurling invective and anathema with an exhaustless energy that could only be of the devil. At length, wheeling suddenly upon me, he said, or rather shrieked, into my face:

"You devils ought to have your heads off, every one of you—do you hear? Do you know that there is an Imperial Edict out for your destruction? You may thank your lucky stars that I don't behead you here and now: indeed, it is only by the greatest stretch of mercy that I spare you."

As he spoke, he suited the action to the word and with the edge of his hand chopped and sawed my neck so violently that it felt tender for hours afterwards. Then, having delivered himself thus, he disappeared within the gate. The virulence of his hate against us went much beyond anything we had yet experienced in the way of *official* malevolence. Our deliverance from death was truly miraculous. A week later, the same Mandarin treated the Saunders-Cooper party from Lucheng to a repetition of the performance but informed them that in exercising the prerogative of mercy he was only restrained by the counter-edict from the Throne issued but a few hours before their arrival cancelling the death order for foreigners. How, then, was it that, with the death order still in force, we were spared?

Thus God wrought for us at Chengchow. We were neither put to death nor sent back to Shansi. But we were packed off to the next county with as little delay as possible. The Mandarin's deputy even softened to the extent of making a gift to the children of 500 cash each.

The treatment we received at the next yamen, Sin-cheng, was a gracious contrast to the terrors of Chengchow. The Mandarin himself, it is true, refused to see us, but his chief secretary was exceedingly kind in the matter of our irregular safe-conduct pass. He prepared a document for us as near as possible equivalent to the coveted passport. Thereafter, we were forwarded from yamen to yamen without the passport being questioned again: Sincheng to Huchow, Huchow to Yinling, Yinling to Yencheng, Yencheng to Siping and Siping to Kiohshan.

We had now reached the period of fiercest heat and right till the end of our journeyings we had to face the "dog days" of the abnormally hot summer. We were passed from one city to another for the next nine days until we reached Sinyang, on the border of the province of Hupeh. All this time we were prisoners and treated as such. At every yamen the rumours we had heard at Wuchih were confirmed, so that we were kept in a perpetual state of uncertainty as to what to expect at each place. Every time we came within sight of a new city we cried to God to keep us in peace, if it were His will, and every time we left a yamen safely on the next stage of our journey we raised a fresh Ebenezer of praise. There were always "perils in the city" and "perils in the wilderness". For the first part of the time, the edict from the Throne for the killing of all foreigners trying to escape was still in force. The rigours of the long day's journey in the heat were invariably followed by the tumultuous and some-times angry reception of the city crowds and an all too short night's rest. Generally speaking, it was a time of hanging in simple faith upon God and there were times when we were as conscious of the Divine environing as Elisha in Dothan or Paul in Corinth.

At the close of our long day's weary ride, we were usually lodged either in the guard room or in a cell immediately adjoining that occupied by convicts. The clanking of their fetters indicated their whereabouts before our eyes became sufficiently accustomed to the gloom to see them: and then how sad and revolting was the sight! We were, however, spared the fate, meted out to some of our brethren, of being thrown in among the convicts.

One such guard room stands out before me with peculiar distinctness. I remember the utter weariness and bodily distress of our condition, when we were driven into the huge yamen courtyard where the swarming thousands immediately hemmed us in. It was one of those occasions when the runners and soldiers failed to make any impression on the mob until the bamboo rods were brought into use. We were at last shown to our resting place for the night: a dark, low-ceilinged room, at the further end of which was a kind of cage. Through the bars we saw the eerie faces of the victims of crime peering at us and laughing with the gaoler over the latest addition to their numbers in the person of "foreign devils". In our state of exhaustion, the noise and the stench were insufferable and we made an appeal, on the ground of my wife's critical state of health, for a change of quarters.

To our intense relief, the runner who took the appeal returned with the good news that the bursar himself would see us. So Miss Gates and I sallied forth by lantern light to the interview. We were kindly received and removed to another part of the prison. There, though the roof was half off, we had the unspeakable comfort of being alone, in quietness and fresh air. We were by no means always so fortunate.

One thing we had occasion to be thankful for—we were never put in irons. Once we were actually warned that at the next city a notorious magistrate would certainly put us in chains. But it did not so happen.

Yet our experiences were occasionally lit up by signal acts of sympathy and kindness. Three times the children were sent for by one or another of the Mandarins' wives and treated with great kindness. On one of these occasions, Miss Gates was allowed to accompany them to the official apartments; on the other two they were summoned alone. These were orders and our hearts sank as they left us, but they were well treated and soon back with us again. At one yamen, the ladies were so charmed with the "foreign children" that a proposal was actually made for their adoption! They always returned with gifts of choice confectionery and strings of cash. On yet another occasion we were actually honoured with a visit in our prison quarters from the Mandarin's lady and her family and suite. There was no fuss of any kind. They behaved quite naturally and sat down on the chairs provided in the courtyard. The rich hues of their embroidered silks and the bright coloured garments of the three children contrasted strangely with our own forlorn appearance and squalid surroundings. But the girls, the eldest being about ten, were delighted to see real live foreign children. After the first shyness, the eldest took Hedley and Hope by the hand and began to chat to them in Chinese. Alas our children's usual merry laugh and dancing smile had faded away through the many days of terror, pain and privation. Their wan, pinched faces looked as if they could never laugh again, but a parting gift from their big friend of some sweetmeats did just succeed in evoking the faintest suspicion of a smile. So kindly was this good lady disposed to us that later in the evening she sent the children a further gift of money and—most welcome of all—a wadded quilt to sleep on. A yamen lady in another place similarly sent a quilt to my wife—an answer to one of our prayers. Thus we began to accumulate a small bundle of things we could call our own. Perhaps the most serviceable thing about it was to provide something soft to sit on in place of the bare boards of the cart and barrow.

The treatment dealt out to us by the Mandarins of these various cities left the impression that they were only anxious to pass the responsibility for us on to the next magistrate as quickly as possible. For this reason, we were almost invariably refused an audience.

On arrival at Kiohshan on July 24th the famous altered telegram had just been received. In this telegram an Imperial order reading "The foreigners must be killed: the foreigners retiring must still be killed" was courageously changed by two officials to "The foreigners must be protected: the foreigners retiring must still be protected". But the Mandarin was most unpleasant and the next day, after providing us vile accommodation, he sent us on, not by cart, but by wheelbarrow. For the next three days we travelled under conditions compared to which even the cart was comfort. Not only so, but we were sent off without so much as the prison allowance for food for the road—thirty cash per head—the only instance where we were so deprived.

Barrow travelling under ordinary conditions can be not only tolerable, but agreeable. But where you have no control of times or stops, no choice of barrowmen or inns, and are in the physical condition in which we were, it is appalling. The barrow is propelled by two men, one in the shafts pushing, the other pulling on ropes in front. Two passengers occupy a narrow board on either side of a large wheel from which they are protected by a wooden encasement. They face backwards and have very little room for their legs and must on no account move lest they disturb the balance of the barrow. There may or may not be a small awning overhead. The great feature of the barrow, however, is the screeching of the ungreased wheel! No barrow man would ever dream of running a silent barrow and the hideous din is the hallmark of his profession.

It was in this way that we travelled for three long days, stopping at intervals to sip water or eat a slice of melon at a wayside booth and to stretch our legs for a few minutes. Better still, to throw ourselves on the ground to ease the aching stiffness. Time and again my poor wife and Miss Gates just dropped in utter weariness from the barrow where it stopped and lay themselves down there. On arrival at our destination, and once installed in our prison quarters, our first concern was always for boiled drinking water and food. But we often had to wait for hours even for these things. Water in anything like sufficient quantities for a good wash was a luxury of which we had dreamed but which we were still not to enjoy. There were occasions when all five of us had to share one basin of water—and this after a day in the intense heat.

Through my wife's constant care, the children's sunburn gradually healed and had ceased to trouble them by the time we reached Sinyang. Since reaching Honan our food situation had eased considerably too. We fed mostly on either dry rice or rice gruel, sometimes with eggs or soya bean curd to go with it. For delicacies, there was an occasional water melon or cucumber, both of which grow locally. The leaves of our "tea" seemed to be of beech or elm. When this was not available, we were glad to drink from the well or the water butt in defiance of the rules of hygiene. On one occasion, we were so thirsty that we accepted "tea" at a wayside shanty which I thought to be putrid, though the others in their thirst had noticed nothing.

As for our escorts, they varied. They were not invariably harsh and on occasions even showed a rough geniality towards the children, with whom they would play and joke as we jolted along. Some of the soldiers became real friends to us and would do anything they could to help us and to protect us from the crowds.

Thus we passed on through the length of beautiful and fearful Honan, until we came in God's safe keeping to the border city of Sinyang.

CHAPTER TWENTY-ONE

CHRIST'S HOSPITAL

OUR arrival at Sinyang was on July 26th, three weeks to a day after our second flight from Luan. But another three weeks lay ahead of us before we were really free from captivity.

As we jolted through the streets and were trundled on our barrows into the great yamen enclosure, the usual multitude was there to push and stare. We were set down just within the gate. Presently two yamen gentlemen in faultless silks made their way through the crowd with the help of runners and stood before us. Addressing me politely, the younger of the two said:

"What is your country? Are you English?"

I could hardly believe my ears. The question was asked in my own tongue! No one can imagine the joy that filled us and the hope that welled up in our hearts at the sound. I almost forgot my Chinese manners so much as to seize his hand, but prudence prevailed and with the orthodox bow, I said:

"Oh, sir, do you speak English? We are indeed from England and we trust you can help us in our misery!"

"Please come this way," he replied. "Follow me."

And through the midst of the wondering multitude we passed within the gates of the second enclosure into an inner and smaller courtyard. Here were gathered a fair-sized group of lesser officials who gave us a reception that quite broke me down. Great sympathy was expressed and sympathy too that took a very practical form. The food set before us included foreign biscuits, sweets and lump sugar! A barber was called and for the first time for three weeks a razor passed over my face and head and a comb through my queue. When I came back, my wife scarcely knew me, so clean and emaciated was I looking.

The normal procedure of official questions completed, we were taken to our quarters—not the prison, nor the guard room, but a small temple standing in a courtyard of its own. The east room was assigned to the guard and the rooms on the other sides were left unoccupied. Our party was ushered into the shrine itself—a roomy enough place, but full of idols and dingy drapery, hung with cob-webbed dirt. Incense sticks still smouldered in the bronze bowls and on the incense table—the only item of furniture there. The floor was of beaten earth, uneven and unswept. The long lattice work of the window frames on either side of the door was stripped of paper, though for this we were grateful as it was our only source of light and ventilation.

Our room was, in spite of everything, a princely place, by comparison, but the chief charm about it for us was its seclusion. By the Mandarin's orders the gate was kept shut and no one from outside the yamen was admitted without special permission. Alone and undisturbed, we were free to enjoy to the full the strange freedom to rest, for which we had long yearned. Rest is again a comparative term, because no provision was made for our comfort: not even a stool to sit on. Our chair was the ground and our bed mother earth!

The next day we were told that there were to be troops

passing through on their way to Peking to oppose the advance of the allied forces and that therefore we were to be detained for our own safety. Anxious as we were to press on, we recognized God's overruling hand in this delay, as my wife was precariously weak and in need of a respite from constant travel. We thus spent eight days in Sinyang, of which five were of almost unrelieved monotony. Apart from an occasional visit from our English-speaking friend we were left strictly to ourselves.

So, to beguile the hours, we arranged a daily routine, particularly for the children's benefit. We began and ended the day with family prayers. After breakfast we set about spring-cleaning our "home" and this was a lengthy business. The children thoroughly enjoyed sweeping the floors with an old broom we found. We took long rests at specified times. With only one hand bowl and one comb between us, it took the five of us some time to complete the daily toilet. The remainder of the time was given to singing and telling stories to the children or making toy mule litters out of odd bits of wood we found in the yard.

From day to day, some little token or other of kindly remembrance was sent from the Mandarin. Once it was a bottle of ginger wine for the ladies; another time it was a bottle of lemonade; another, about a teaspoonful of ground coffee. The coffee was eked out, a pinch at a time, in our breakfast cup of hot water. The third day, a large parcel was sent round containing five sets of brand new blue cloth garments, a set apiece! So now at last—the first time for just upon a month—we elders had a change of raiment.

Two other incidents of those first five days are written

on my memory. The fifth day was a Sunday and so we held a morning service in our temple prison, the first and only occasion during our flight on which we were able to worship without distraction. Hymn books, prayer books, Bibles we had none. But a happier hour of fellowship with God we had seldom experienced. The other incident is worthy of record. The Mandarin's four-year-old little son was sent to the temple the same day with a couple of maids to prostrate himself before the god. But when it came to the moment, he absolutely refused and nothing could persuade him to perform this act of worship. The maids went off wondering whatever had come over the child, as he had never behaved like this before. They knew not that the Lord was there.

The following day, July 30th, we were officially informed that a large party of foreigners was expected to arrive that evening and that they were to share our quarters. We did not know who they might be, but were filled with eager expectation. We thought it might well be the friends from Lucheng and how eagerly and busily we made ready to welcome them, dressing up in our new gowns in their honour! In due course we heard the sound of carts rumbling into the yard and we went out to welcome whomsoever it might be.

Shall I ever forget the sight? Slowly and painfully they were descending from the carts, a company of twelve— three men, four women and five children. One by one they appeared in their rags, emaciation and utter woebegoneness, more like apparitions than flesh and blood. Our surmise was correct: it was the Lucheng-Pingyao party. Mrs. E. J. Cooper was the first to come forward,

My dear wife ran to her and with a tender embrace led her gently in. Next came her husband, his arms round a litter of straw; then Mr. A. R. Saunders and Mr. A. Jennings in like manner. These were followed by the ladies—Mrs. Saunders, Miss Huston and Miss Guthrie, leading or carrying the children, though scarcely able to support their own weight.

They passed within the enclosure to their temple quarters; and stretching themselves on the ground, as we had done five days before, gave thanks to God for the reviving of His grace in the rest provided after weeks of torture. The earth-floor of our room was now covered, every yard of it, with sick and wounded. Some had open wounds, caused either by the sun or by the galling of the limbs on the carts, others were suffering from dysentery. Miss Huston had a broken jaw and a gaping scalp wound, the work of the Boxers. The children all had dysentery and undressed sunburn wounds, some of them gangrened and alive with maggots. Two of the party were missing: baby Isobel Saunders had succumbed to the hardships of the flight and Miss Rice had been murdered outright by the Boxers at Tsehchow.

Little by little we gleaned, with fresh wonder and amazement, the details of their escape—details that only emphasized the conviction that they, not less than we, had been brought forth by a definite act of Almighty purpose and power.

With our numbers swollen thus from five to seventeen, and under such insanitary conditions, our small room became more like a pest house than a hospital. Medical resources we had none. Outside, just beneath the window, the only latrine for the use of us all became offensive in the extreme in the fierce heat.

The day after the arrival of the large party, Miss Gates succeeded in securing a Chinese antiseptic of some sort and set to work cleansing the wounds with a cold solution. The process, in the case of the dear children, was distressing, for to them it gave the sensation of being scalded with boiling water. The cries of pain told severely on nerves already sorely strained. Nor was there any respite night or day. By day the process of washing, dressing the wounds, laundering the clothes and cooking for the sick kept the more able-bodied busy. Everyone found the least exertion exhausting and the sense of utter weakness was overwhelming. Not the least hardship was the lack of any privacy except that provided by two small recesses, of which the ladies were glad.

Several kind inquiries about our welfare were made by the Mandarin and gifts of clothing, food and money sent for the new arrivals. Occasional groups of city gentry, too, were allowed admittance; but nothing would induce them to step inside our evil-smelling room.

Day after day we inquired about the prospects of continuing our journey and entreated to be allowed to be sent forward at the earliest opportunity. But we were constantly told that the road was not yet clear of troops. And so we waited on. Under suffering of the most distressing kind, not one single syllable of murmur or complaint fell from the lips of any. Even the children never said a word of distrust of the love of God nor questioned His way with them. The ministry of mutual cleansing in the lowly "washing of one another's feet" was most graciously exemplified and beautiful to see. No man sought his own, but each man his neighbour's good. A tender-heartedness, the outcome of meek submission to the known will of God, breathed through all our relations with one another, infusing into them withal a certain cheerfulness that killed irritability in the germ. Even there, amid so much that tended to wretchedness, we were given "beauty for ashes, the oil of joy for mourning, the garment of praise for the spirit of heaviness". To Him be glory for ever. Amen.

CHAPTER TWENTY-TWO

JOURNEY'S END

ON the ninth day of our detention in Sinyang, Friday, August 3rd, the good news came that the road was clear of soldiers and that we could proceed on our journey. Our hopes had sunk very low and conditions in our place of detention were sapping the very springs of life.

The plans made for our journey were, however, a bitter disappointment. Nothing better than barrows could be provided for our transport. The Mandarin had intended to arrange chairs for the stronger and stretchers for the weaker amongst us, but the passing troops had commandeered every chair and requisitioned every chair-bearer. Stretchers could easily be improvised but bearers were not so easily replaced. Two stretchers only were therefore available for Mrs. Cooper and Mrs. Saunders. The rest of us, whatever our condition, were to have nothing but barrows.

Despite our disappointment and the prospect of another painful journey, we were all glad to be on the move again and full of praise to God for having provided such a place as the temple we had just left for our partial convalescence. The Mandarin and others had been most kind and we said farewell to them and to Sinyang with mixed feelings.

How strange it seemed, after nine days' seclusion, to pass out again to the bustle of the great yamen square where we made ourselves as comfortable as possible on our conveyances. That first day was just a repetition of many similar days: heat, coarse food, surly barrowmen and the interminable jolt and bang as we screeched on our way. What made things rather worse than usual was the fact that all of us were now suffering from dysentery, my wife by this time being greatly weakened as a result of the long continuance of the disease.

We were unable to cover the whole distance to Yingshan in one day and so had to spend the night at a village called Tankinho. Half of us were shown to a large barrow shed and the rest were taken to an inn higher up the street. In the mercy of God, our arrival seemed to excite nothing beyond ordinary curiosity and we prepared to spend the night as best we could, in our case, in the barrow shed where we spread out our quilt on the ground between the barrows.

We were not yet asleep when, about ten o'clock, the startling news was brought down from the inn that little Jessie Saunders was dead! Prostrate as we knew her to have been, there had been nothing to call for immediate apprehension, so that the news came as a great shock, the more so as this was the first appearance of death in our midst. I immediately walked to the inn through the deserted streets. There, outside in the street in the moonlight, was the sweet form of Jessie lying on a rush mat. The landlord, according to superstitious custom, had had her carried out there to die. Beside her sat the stricken mother, in calm resignation to the will of Him who was calling her for His sake to part with her eldest, so soon after He had asked for her youngest.

The arrangements for the funeral were made quickly, the officer in charge of the escort giving most valuable assistance. The little grave was dug on a hillside outside the village gate and at sunrise, Jessie was laid to rest by her sorrowing father in the land of her short life's affliction.

As rumours of more soldiery approaching were about, the escort ordered an early start for Yingshan, in order to get there before the soldiers did. This new danger called for earnest prayer for protection. The haste meant longer intervals between the halts and so longer periods of torture on the barrows and in the heat. In spite of this we feared almost as much to stop as to go on. As the morning advanced, we learned from passers-by that the vanguard of five battalions had already passed through Yingshan and that we would meet them soon. We halted at noon for a meal of rice gruel and it was while we were halted that the soldiers, who were from Wuchang, descended on the village.

When they found who we were, a great commotion ensued and these men who were on their way to the capital "to drive the 'foreign devils' into the Yellow Sea" were eager to start their task there and then. But our escort discharged their responsibilities faithfully and the army officers recognized that we were under arrest and restrained their men from any lawless action. The troops finished their rice and marched on. But not before Miss Huston had been roughly handled and Miss Gates dragged from her seat by her hair. Mrs. Cooper and Mrs. Saunders in their stretchers were some way behind the rest of the party when the soldiers met them. Their bearers set down the stretchers and ran. The two sick women were prodded with the butt end of muskets but were otherwise unmolested.

The rest of the journey to Yingshan was increasingly rough going and things were made worse by the cruelty of the barrowmen and, in the case of our family, their refusal at one point to go any further. When they did proceed it was to aggravate the normal painful progress over a paved way of stone slabs by deliberately keeping the barrows out of the well-worn wheel track and crashing us over the roughest parts of the road. My wife suffered terribly and as for little Hope, her nerve power seemed quite gone and she sobbed continuously with terror.

At long last we arrived at Yingshan, again not knowing what kind of a reception to expect. But, as we turned up the narrow street leading to the yamen, a gentleman made his way towards us with the common Christian greeting of "Peace!" In a moment, the dreadful tension of the day relaxed in the knowledge that we were in friendly hands. At the yamen, the Mandarin himself and some lesser officials were waiting to receive us and—to our great surprise—to greet us with an English handshake! With a few kindly words, he led us to the ante-room of his own private apartments where a lounge and several easy chairs were placed at our disposal. The Christian who had greeted us on the street came in and spoke to the Mandarin and we knew that all was working out for our good. Tea and biscuits were served and my wife who had fainted with heat and exhaustion was given wine to revive her. Then we were accommodated in a small orphanage where we were to spend another six days because of the continued movement of troops.

We now found that we were the guests of Christians connected with the London Missionary Society and Mr. Lo's ministry to us during our stay was a noble instance of lowly, self-sacrificing service, after the mind and the pattern of Christ. No task was too menial for him, none too disagreeable. Patiently and tenderly, he made himself the least of all and the servant of all.

Each day we hoped to continue our journey. Each day we were doomed to disappointment. We were all weak and ill and desperately needed to reach Hankow for medical attention if we were all to survive. My wife appeared to be sinking and Mrs. Saunders was also desperately ill with dysentery.

On the third day of our stay, August 6th, Mrs. E. J. Cooper passed away. In the morning nothing seemed to indicate that the end was near, but about two o'clock she showed signs of distress and shortly afterwards with the words, "Rest, rest, rest!" she was gone. The Mandarin courteously arranged for the removal of the body to Hankow for interment.

On the morning of August 10th, we took a thankful farewell of our most sad abode, but Mr. Lo accompanied us, resolving not to leave us until he had fulfilled his ministry in bringing us to Hankow itself. We spent the next night at Tehan where we were lovingly tended by a Chinese doctor of the Wesleyan Mission and on the following day we pursued our way to Yünmeng arriving about three in the afternoon.

It was here that another of the martyrs passed to heaven's perfect peace. Miss Huston became perceptibly worse after our arrival and towards evening Mr. Saunders summoned me to be with her as she too finished her course. Here again, as at Yingshan, the kindness of the Mandarin made matters easy, and permission was granted to take the remains with us to Hankow.

One hundred miles still lay between us and our destination. This might take four days and how we were to endure this last long stage we did not know. We started off again on Sunday, August 12th, and more than once that day I thought my dear wife was dying. But she revived and we safely reached Hsiaokan about midday and were very warmly received and cared for by the Chinese Christians connected with the London Missionary Society. Every attention was given to our wants, the sick and wounded being lovingly tended in the mission dispensary. We were served with the most delicious meals, and for the children there was diluted condensed milk in abundance.

That evening we embarked on boats to make the remainder of the journey by river. It was a new and wonderful experience to be travelling and yet not to be conscious of it! But the heat was intense, night and day. So prostrate was my wife that I continually feared for her life. Hedley, too, lay very ill; and I had to attend to them the whole time. Twenty-four hours brought us, almost unexpectedly, to Hankow with its maze of river-craft on the mighty Yangtse and its Han tributary.

Could it be that the impossible was actually realized? Had God indeed brought us up from the gates of death and turned our thousand miles of peril into His thousand miles of miracle? With hearts bowed in adoration, we gave thanks to Him that liveth for ever and ever, the only wise God, *our Saviour*.

Owing to the dilatoriness of the local official, we were not taken off the boat until the next day. We watched in vain for the chairs which never came. The long night vigil on board beside my wife and son, both at death's door, came to an end with the dawn. There, on the wharf, was Mr. Lewis Jones of the China Inland Mission, accompanied by Dr. Gillison of the London Missionary Society and Dr. Hall of the Methodist Episcopal Mission, to render us the most loving and helpful service.

The news that a party of missionaries had arrived from Shansi created quite a sensation in Hankow, because it was the common belief that none had lived to cross the Yellow River. The British Consul, Mr. Fraser, and Mr. Brown, the American Consul, were foremost in the practical expression of their delight at our safe arrival, while Dr. Griffith John, the patriarch of foreign missions in Hankow, gave us the tenderest welcome in the Lord. The next day we said goodbye to Mr. Lo of Yingshan as he returned to his work. He took with him a small subscription from us all in token of our love, esteem and gratitude.

In the early morning hours of August 18th, the fourth day after our arrival at Hankow, my wife gave birth to a living child. The fact that the little one breathed was regarded by the doctors as no less a miracle than that the mother should have lived to bring her into the world.

But after six days the baby turned from her food and on the tenth day the little life ended. Two weeks later my wife and the other two children, who had also been critically ill, were thought well enough to travel to Shanghai by river steamer. At Shanghai a most affectionate welcome awaited us from the mission's leaders; and friends from many other missions expressed their sympathy with us in a most generous manner. On September 19th my wife suffered a relapse and, after lingering through five more weeks of suffering, lovingly ministered to by Dr. F. H. Judd and the nurses, she went to be with Christ on October 25th, at the age of twenty-eight. Over all the unspeakable sorrow was the heavenly consolation that the deepest longings of her soul were now satisfied, for God was with her, her God, and had wiped away all tears from her eyes. She was the last of the martyrs of 1900 to pass from the cross to the crown.

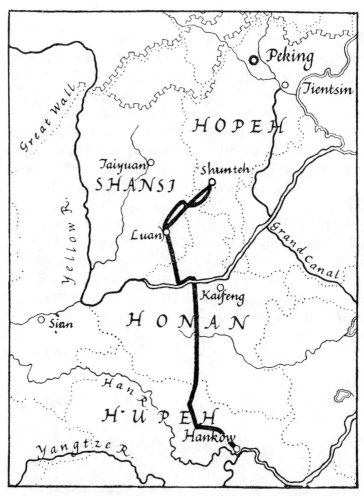

Showing the route taken by Mr. Glover's party: first from Luan to Shunteh, then from Shunteh, via Luan, to Hankow on the Yangtze, and then eastwards by boat to Shanghai.